Lettermorphosis

Poetry By
Daren Peary

Illustration by
Daniel G. Rodriguez

AN M-Y BOOKS PAPERBACK

© Copyright 2016
Daren Peary

A CIP catalogue record for this title is
available from the British Library

ISBN–978-1-911124-20-7

CONTENTS

PARADISE

THIS IS THE BEST DAY OF THE YEAR,
DOWN THE SLITHERING LANES IN HERTFORDSHIRE.
WHITE STUBBS VALLEY WHERE HORSES GRAZE.
AT PARADISE WILDLIFE PARK YOU WILL BE AMAZED.

THE FAMILY ZOO WITH A SMILEY CULTURE,
BIRDS OF PREY AND MAYBE A VULTURE.
SOME OF THE ANIMALS ARE NOW QUITE RARE,
AND THATS A GOOD REASON TO GO THERE.

TO HELP WITH THE CONSERVATION FIGHT,
GO ALONG AND YOU JUST MIGHT,
WATCH THE MONKEYS JUMPING AROUND,
TAKE THE CHILDREN, WITH SO MUCH FUN TO BE FOUND.

MY FAVOURITE IS THE TIGER WITH EYES BURNING BRIGHT,
THE POWER AND THE COLOURS ARE OUT OF SIGHT.
YOU CAN ALWAYS GET UP CLOSE AND FEEL THE BREATH,
WE MUST PROTECT THEM FROM THIS UNNATURAL DEATH.

I CANNOT SIT BACK AND WATCH NUMBERS DIMINISH,
I JUST WANT THE FOREST DESTRUCTION TO FINISH.
I WANT TO BE ABLE TO LOOK INTO HIS EYES,
WITH HONESTY, FAITH AND NO COMPROMISE.

WE MUST SHOW COMPASSION FOR ALL THE ANIMALS HERE ON EARTH
AND MAKE A STAND FOR WHAT IT'S WORTH.
JUST THINK OF A LAND THAT IS TIGER-FREE,
THE BARREL OF THE GUN MUST BE EMPTY.

THE LION, CECIL, WE ALL CHERISHED,
THE LIGHTS WENT OUT WHEN HE PERISHED.
WE MUST STOP THE CRUELTY, MAKE AN OUTRIGHT BAN,
YOU ARE A FOOL, MR HUNTER MAN.

AS TIME PASSES BY AND WE WATCH THE DIAL,
I WANT TO SEE THE TIGER SMILE.
I WANT TO SEE THE LION ROAR,
I WANT TO HELP: I WANT TO DO MORE.

I WANT TO SEE THE PENGUINS SWIM,
I WANT TO SEE THEIR EYES BRIGHT NOT DIM.
I WANT TO SEE THE BIRDS FLY NORTH AND SOUTH,
I WANT TO SEE THE CROCODILE'S MOUTH.

I WANT TO SEE HOPE AND BLUE SKIES,
I WANT TO LOOK INTO THE TIGER'S EYES.
I WANT TELL HIM "IT'S OK, WE CARE."
I WANT TO TELL HIM HE IS NOT RARE.

I WANT TO MAKE THE OCEANS BLUE,
I WANT TO SEND THIS MESSAGE TO YOU.
MANKIND LISTEN UP, THIS IS YOUR BIG CHANCE,
ITS TIME TO DO THE TIGER DANCE.

GUARDIAN OF THE FOREST, YOU GIVE ME SO MUCH PLEASURE,
YOU REALLY ARE THE WORLD'S HIDDEN TREASURE.
WITH EYES ON PREY AND EYES ON YOU,
PLEASE FORGIVE THEM AND WHAT THEY DO.

IF THERE WAS ONE THING THAT I WAS BORN TO DO,
IT MUST BE TO PROTECT YOU.
SO DON'T JUST HIDE AWAY IN THE DARK,
PAY A VISIT TO PARADISE WILDLIFE PARK.

LYNN AND HER CREW ARE AN INSPIRATION,
JUMP ON THE BUS AND WITHOUT HESITATION.
LOOK INTO THE TIGER'S EYES,
A PERFECT DAY,
YOU'LL BE SURPRISED!

MY WORLD

Welcome to my world, it's a little upside down,
All the bats stand up and the cows all sit down.
White is the new black and black is often white,
Night is in the day and day is always night,
All the poor are rich and all the rich are poor,
More is sometimes less and less is much, much more.
When everything is fast, I like going slow,
When its time to stop, I will always go.
All the old are young and the young are never old,
When it's really hot I am always cold.
The sick are not sick but are healthy all the time,
There's no such thing as money and never any crime.
The sad are always happy and the happy never sad,
All the bad are good and the good are never bad.
It's a little bit confusing but it's my world after all,
Everything that's big is really very small.
The weather is always lovely and the rain goes up not down,
The people are all nice and it's my kinda town.
I'm never ever wrong – in fact I'm always right,
I often go to work in the middle of the night.
All the tears are dry and all the laughter shared,
The hospitals are empty cos all the caring cared.
The sky is always blue and the clouds are seldom seen,
The grass is all pink and all the people green.
When you go in sometimes you come out,
I really do not know what my world is all about.
The animals are all loved and we do not kill a thing,
There are still the birds that tweet and I love it when they sing.
There is no such thing as greed cos there's always more and plenty,

When the box looks full up it's sometimes rather empty.
All the hatred turns to love and the love grows day by day,
So you can come into my world cos you won't have to pay.
The music plays quite loud but at times you can hear the breeze,
All the colds have gone and you never ever sneeze.
Laughter fills the streets and there is colour everywhere,
The artist does his art and the politicians leave,
The thing about my world is that it's a place that I believe.
So I'm not going to say goodbye – in fact it's a warm hello,
I might be sitting all alone but at least my world can grow.
The greatest thing of all in my world that it's full of dreams,
The rivers are all clean and there are fish in all the streams.
The sun is always smiling and the moon is made of cheese,
There are whales and dolphins swimming – in fact they own the seas.
The future looks quite good in my world and that is bad,
Because instead of feeling happy I'm feeling rather sad.
My world is never open – in fact it's closing soon,
With all the hungry children riding on a spoon,
To a world without starvation and where everyone can taste,
The thing about my world is there's never any waste.
So if you want a return ticket then do something upside down,
I will kiss and love and hug you because you're welcome in my town.
And even though I am Biggie, I'm not small at all,
If someone were to push you then I'd catch you when you fall.
It's strange to live in my head and as I said right from the start,
Or was it at the finish when I gave you all my heart?

A FISTFUL OF POEMS

I have got a fistful of poems and a few poems more,
I'm the tongue slinger and my lines are the law,
I have got a wagon of words and I am firing bullets of gold,
I'm on a stagecoach tonight, feeling quite bold,
I'm shooting and looting, I'm the Bard from the yard,
My lyrics will hit you and hit you real hard,
I'm just passing through – some say the new kid in town,
I will lift you all up and take you right down,
I did shoot the sheriff with a couple of lines,
So he paid the price with his bad ugly rhymes,
It was the bittersweet taste, a small price to pay,
So I just gave him a poem and said 'make my day',
It was in the saloon bar that he bit the dust,
He was the man that no one could trust,
I'm quick on the jaw, a bounty headhunter,
With a reward for wanted, a poetry punter,
I'm a big hairy honcho with poncho and pen,
But I've written more poems than I have killed men
I've got these cowboy boots so I am going to strut,
So I went to the bar and they said it was shut,
I'm a rebel, a bandit with a posse to follow,
When I get to the hangman I'm going to holler,
I play Russian roulette with a font then I run,
There is only one reason to load up my gun,
As i look down the barrel with a bag loaded with loot,
I'm going to read out the rhyme then I'm going to shoot,
I'm still spitting the bars as winds blow through the yard,
The timepiece will stop time to play the right card,
Even the good the bad and the ugly will fight you,
There is only a thing that I'm going to write you,
With a gallop of grime and my holster popping
You aren't digging the grave then I'm not into hip-hopping,
Now time to tumble, drag out the boxes
Send in the bandits, let out the foxes,
Send 'em all in, they're here to fetch ya,
Your card game is over – I'm going getcha,
I'm going to finish you off with my bad ugly tunes,
So strike me a match, light my cigar,
I'm leaving town but I ain't going that far,
I'm no Lee Van Cleef or Mr Eastwood,
But my rhymes are sublime and really quite good,
As the train leaves the station I'm jumping on board
I have jumped out of jail and claimed my reward,
With my fistful of poems I head for the station,
And my poncho looks cool – it's my destination,
To head for the hills and ride until dawn,
With a few poems more about to be born.

THE RETURN OF MR C

He has taken more than we hoped for,
He has hung around for too long.
He hunts like a shark in life's oceans,
Somebody has got it all wrong.

Mr C, you are never welcome,
Deep is the scar that you leave.
I'm just saying we are coming to catch you,
And that is what I truly believe.

The net is closing around you,
As the scientists make up the bait.
You might even have one more bite left,
If I were you I just wouldn't wait.

Mr C you are the ultimate predator,
As you hunt on the young and the old.
If I can pick up the pieces to catch you,
Then I know that my treasure is gold.

Sometimes words are better unspoken,
As we recover from the loss and the shock.
We can call it the confusion collective,
As time tears fall from the clock.

Mr C we will hit you with poison,
And take all the life from your veins.
As the hair falls from your shoulders,
Souls taken and no one explains.

When the chair is left cold and empty,
And the morning is filled with a gloom,
My days are now in the moment,
When Mr C walks into the room.

Mr C, I want to punch you and kick you,
For the pain that you cause in our world.
I cannot find explanations,
I can remember the hand that I held.

Sometimes the sadness overwhelms us,
But we continue to search for the clues.
We must shout from the rooftops we hate you,
To prevent all the Mr C blues.

If Mr C arrives on your doorstep,
And tries to enter with a fast pace,
Just tell him he has not been invited,
And slam the door in his face.

Let all the charity and research continue,
And lets put Mr C up to bed.
And hope he don't wake in the morning,
And hear the words that I've said.

Mr C, you have not been a good boy,
In fact the worst in the class.
If I could teach you one special lesson,
I'd smash you to pieces like glass.

The oceans are better without you,
Although you have taken some close to me.
The land it is greener and brighter,
And the skies are as blue as the seas.

I'm going to give Mr C this little poem,
And send it with love in a sack,
Put him in my special rocket,
And hope that he don't come back.

As the north points its nukes towards the south
the world waits and watches with hands on mouth
I can only but think this is not a game to play
I say I say I say I say
can I have the opportunity
to stop this now it makes no sense to me
to be or not to be in war so give peace a chance
such words gently spoken and life taken
again and again and again
It's insane mad or bad or just rhetoric
a time a place a mask behind a face
a man is brought before the king
to see if anyone is listening
to me or is this just a threat
to keep the world wondering
and yet
I want to try and make things better
I will start by sending them this letter
to all of you in north and south
these words are gifted from my mouth
don't fight don't fight I beg of you
just come to mine for a bbq
we can share and talk about the differences you find
I think it's best for humankind
we can cuddle up and share a glass or two
here's my message to all of you
don't nuke each other
dance together
mr kim jong un I'm inviting you to go that extra mile
chill out bro and let's go gangman style
I don't know how much more we can take
perhaps we can do the harlem shake
shake a leg and shake them hips I don't want a row
I just want peace not apuckerlips now!

BUBBLE

I THINK I'D RATHER LIVE IN A BUBBLE,
AND FLOAT AROUND FOR DAYS.
RELAXING IN THE AIR, IT'S GOOD IN OH SO MANY WAYS.
WATCHING ALL THE COLOURS REFLECTING IN THE LIGHTS,
IT COULD FEEL AMAZING, REACHING MANY HEIGHTS.
UP ABOVE THE TREES, WITH THE BIRDS AND BEES,
SITTING ON MY BUBBLE OR ON MY HANDS AND KNEES.
BEING CAREFUL NOT TO BURST OR LET MY BUBBLE POP,
I WOULDN'T LET MY BUBBLE NEVER, EVER STOP.
I'D GO TO NEVERLAND AND PLAY WITH PIRATES THERE,
YOU COULD COME AND JOIN ME, LIKE WE HAVEN'T GOT A CARE.
WE COULD BUMP INTO EACH OTHER OR SHARE A BUBBLE CLEAR,
WE COULD GO TO BUBBLE LAND, WE WOULDN'T HAVE TO FEAR.
THERE'S SOMETHING ABOUT A BUBBLE THAT FLOATS SO HIGH ABOVE,
I THINK IT'S BECAUSE THEY'RE FRAGILE AND RIDE WITH BLOWS OF LOVE.

BEAUTIFUL

SKIN DEEP AND SWEET INNOCENCE,
YOUR LAUGHTER AND SMILE REACHES ME,
ON THE OTHERSIDE OF THE ROAD.
YOUR HEARTBEAT WARMS ME,
YOUR CHARM CALMS ME.
THE RIVER HEALS ME,
THE CLOCK KILLS ME.
IF LOVE IS BLIND THEN I'M SEEING RIGHT THROUGH IT,
DON'T WAIT FOR ME TO TAKE THE RIGHT TURN.
THERE'S ONE THING YOU NEED TO LEARN ABOUT ME,
THAT'S MY LOVE, IN A ROUNDABOUT WAY.
YOU ARE BEAUTY PERSONIFIED,
DON'T HURT ME.
TAKE MY INSECURITY AND WORK ME.
LOCK IT AWAY IN A BOX FOR A KEEPSAKE,
TONIGHT I'LL KEEP YOU FOREVER HIDDEN IN MY DREAMS.
IT SEEMS THAT YOUR LINGERING TEARS LIKE FEARS,
SPLASH UPON MY SHOULDERS,
AND GET LOST IN A FAIRGROUND FANTASY.
BROKEN PROMISES AND WISHES FLY,
AWAY ON LIP CLOUDS THAT BLOW,
INTO THE DISTANCE.
AND STILL MY HEART BEATS,
I'VE TOUCHED YOUR SHADOW.
NOW YOU,
YOU ARE QUITE SIMPLY,
BEAUTIFUL

THE DOG AND WHISTLE

Mrs Boarder became a hoarder; she couldn't let things go,
When Mrs Boarder made an order she often used Tesco.
Her favourite place was running outta space and now no room to swing a cat,
She loved Brick Lane and although insane preferred to always wear her hat.
Her Nanny B had OCD and that's why we think she's hoarding,
She had fifty clocks and wore pink socks, which she found most rewarding.
Her best friend Hector was a stamp collector and even had a Penny Black,
In his position, it was his ambition to go around the world and back.
Her grandpa Mike had an antique bike and he said it's worth repairing,
He said, "Mmm, it's no tandem and unfortunately not for sharing".
Her auntie Joan had a classic phone, the type you finger dial,
She was a bit of a snob with a wonky gob and you would never see her smile.
Now Mrs Boarder became quite famous all around the town,
Cos she looked a bit of a mess in her Westwood dress,
And she constantly wore a frown.
She was by far, in her padded bra, a lady full of habit,
She got uptight and put up a fight – when she saw it she would have it.
She was past her prime and just in time followed fashion every week,
When her collection had direction, now known as shabby chic.
One day she ventured out to a nice place called the Dog and Whistle,
It didn't take long in the emporium to find a hat that had a thistle.
So without haste she had a taste of their coffee and carrot cake,
She felt at home with time to roam, there must be something she can take.
She felt fulfilled on the Chesterfield as it was brown and made of leather,
She didn't stay long cos she knew it was wrong to stay out in this weather.
Now her auntie Mabel had a mahogany table she thought she might try part-exchange,
But Mrs Boarder is a hoarder and at times appeared quite strange.
Her uncle Jimmy had a classic Mini and she thought it might be worth using,
So I am going to try and explain this to you so stay with it, it gets confusing.
Yes time don't stop in this wonderful shop, the next bit gets quite erotic,
Cos Mrs boarder enjoys a dance and at times is quite robotic.
Now at 7.30 she was feeling flirty and rubbed her hands with joy,
Cos she felt reborn with antique porn and gazed over at Playboy.
Now Mrs Boarder loves her home and cupboards full of clutter,
But in this day and age you can feel the rage and people they all mutter.
So with her fox's fur she caused a stir and looked over at the clock,
It's time to go and so I will purchase another flowery frock.
And so it must be penned – the time has come but let me leave you with this ending,
Mrs Boarder said to me, "Your poetry really is worth sending."
So after some inspection, I now have a vast collection,
Cos Grandpa Bill made a will and she gave him an injection.
She spent ten grand on a second hand vintage camera,
She had the op and now won't swap her classic padded bra.
Mrs Boarder is still a hoarder and there's not a lady finer,
But you can't change that, I love her hat,
But she can keep her fine bone china.
And so if you go to the Dog and Whistle, it's the place to come to eat,
And if you see Mrs Boarder say hello and don't forget to tweet.

ADAM ANT

I was adamant that Adam's aunt was Adam Ant
But now I've seen my ways
I'm not so adamant anymore
And if Adam's aunt was Adam Ant
Then I wouldn't be so adamant, that's for sure.
And I like Adam Ant and I like Adam's aunt
But the two of them together don't rock my boat.
If i found that Adam's aunt was into Adam Ant
Then I might see things differently
Especially if Adam Ant was adamant that they were an item.

MENU FOR A POEM

Ingredients are as follows:

1/2 cup words,
2 spoonfuls of rhyme.
If you don't like it,
Take it out next time.
Spaghetti letters: use for a sauce,
A little pinch of creativity,
Imagination for the first course.
Add a small beat and a give it a mix,
Dash of champers for a quick fizz.
Stick in a handful of herbs,
Maybe a tiny amount of verbs,
Paper and pen or something to write,
Leave in fridge perhaps overnight.
You might want to put it in a rap,
Keep it together – use a nice bap.
Some might use drama or props,
A pound of thoughts until the penny drops.
Weigh it all up and write it all down,
Add colour and scent,
Or throw in a noun.
Season it well with pepper and salt,
Maybe stick in a splash of old malt.
Glass of wine will do the job,
I like mine with corn on the cob.
A poetry pie is my treat,
Just for you I'll add some heat.
Passion and pain, laughter and tears,
It will probably last for a couple of years.
Pop in the oven,
Decide when to read it,
Even though you probably don't need it.
Gobble it up – I've made quite a few,
This the recipe for my poetry stew.
Let's make it big – as big as a car.
Maybe I'll get a Michelin star.

HOMELESS

My friends are the birds that sing to me as each day dawns,
My thoughts are still with you with each memory reborn.
I'm empty inside yet full of this rage,
Nothing means everything, so I'll turn the page.
Some are now with, some left without,
Sometimes I don't know what life is about.
The time has no meaning, each minute filled with despair,
The forgotten generation in a world that don't care,
My dreams are too cloudy because you are not there,
I know it is easy to turn the other cheek,
But sometimes I wonder will I be alive this time next week.
The indulgence of you means someone will die,
All that I hear is another grand lie.
As I head for the arches with tin grasped in my hand,
My soul has forgotten that this is my land.
Old Father Thames guides me and destiny awaits,
Am I bound for the Tower or bound to the gates?
The memories fade and the drinking kicks back,
I'm the one with this burden to crack.
As all pity subsides and gets lost in the fog,
Suddenly I'm greeted by a barking dog.
I didn't choose this, it chose me,
Abused by ignorance, misconception and mutual aggression.
I'm all there is, me my only possession.
So now I've lost you...

I've lost my children and I've lost my wife
I've nothing, I have only my life.
That is something, I suppose.
I have lost the roof that covered my head,
One day when you read this, I will be dead.
I didn't want this to burden your mind,
It is the way of humankind.
Thank you for the string in my boots,
I used to wear those trendy blue suits.
There's dampness in my clothes, there's holes in my shoes,
I might as well jump: I've got nothing to lose.
Having you with me will set me free,
You would never believe what has happened to me.
As you stare upon me as if I was trash,
The only thing you can give me is cash.
I was pissed on by dogs on the corner of Poetry Street,
Perhaps in the next life we could all meet.
I laugh at the people who race like rats in the town,
I'm known as the ol' fool, the city clown.
Homeless, why? All because of the government cuts,
The cuts go deeper than you think,
I didn't even have time to blink.
The 'Please Help' sign that you read is certainly true,
All that I have is this message for you.
I am a person, you have nothing to fear,
So perhaps this time you will lend me your ear.
I once was like you, so do not judge me, it just isn't fair,
I am a statistical reminder and I know you don't care.

Not a Strawberry not a Raspberry
not a Blackberry not a Logonberry
not a Halley Berry not a French berry
not a London berry not a Blueberry
not a Bilberry not a Cranberry
not an Elderberry not a Younger berry
not a Hooseberry not a Huckleberry
not a Mulberry not a Bear berry (that's me)
i want to be a Glastonbury xx
any free tickets?

A SPACE COMMODITY

I AM NOT A SPACEMAN IN THIS PLACEMAN
AS THINGS GO AND IM BLOWING BUBBLES AT THE HUBBELLS
AND IM MORE HEINZ IN THAN EINSTEIN
COSMICALLY COMICAL AND I WOULDNT CALL MYSELF AN INSTER STELLA FELLA
I THINK IM ASTROPHOBIC AND HAVE NO BIG BANG THEORY
IM MORE MINI MOUSE THAN MAJOR TOM AND HAVE NO BOMBS TO DROP ON
MORE OF A BIKER THAN GALAXY HITCH HIKER
WITH NO SHIP TO GUIDE ME OR HIDE ME ITS WHATS INSIDE THIS MIND OF MINE
SUPERHUMAN NOT A BLUESMAN EXPLORING THIS UNIVERSE
IM TELESCOPICALLY TUNED IN AND ALSO WATCHING THE MOON MEN
MORE HARMLESS THAN ARMSTRONG WITH A STARBURST
IVE GOT MORE PAUNCH IN MY LAUNCHPAD AND IM STARING AT CRATERS
MY PLANETS ALIGNED BUT MY METEORITE IS SOMETIMES WRONG
IVE GOT A STRONG FEELING ABOUT THE BLACK HOLE
IM SORRY TO SAY ITS MY FLAG UP THE FLAGPOLE
IVE GOT MORE IN MY POCKET THAN A ROCKET WITH LIGHT SPEED
CAPTAIN OF THE STARS AND IM GLOATING WHILST FLOATING ON A TIN CAN
MORE GASTRO THAN ASTRO AND NOT A MOON MADE MARTIAN
GRAVITATIONALLY GROTESQUE WITH A BEE IN MY HELMET
BUZZING ON AIR AND MY SPACESUIT IS VELVET
WITH ALL THIS COSMIC INFLATION IM FALLING WITH HEIGHT FEARS
THE LIGHT YEARS ARE GLOWING AND IM RACING THE PACEMAN
I AM NOT A SPACEMAN BUT IAM TALKING TO HAWKING AND WALKING ON SUNSHINE
SOME SAY DIMENSIONALLY DELUDED MORE OF A WORD MAN THAN A BIRD MAN
MORE BOOTS ON THAN NEWTON WITH A RAYGUN
LIVE IN MY SEVERE WORLD NOT A SPHERE WORLD
WAITNG FOR THE CATAUSTRAPHPHIC TO CATCH ME
ECLIPSING THE COMETS USING CELESTIAL MECHANICS TO HATCH ME
I PUT THE FUN IN FUNDAMENTAL AND RUDELY RUDIMENTAL
AN AIR DE FAMILLE WITH NO SHOULDER TO CRY ON
MORE CRYING THAN FLYING TO FREEDOM
NOT DARK MATTER OR LIGHT NO MATTER WHAT IT DONT MATTER
MORE PHYSICAL THAN PHYSICS AND MORE LYRICAL IN BUSINESS
A SPACE COMMODITY VOLUNTARILY BREAKING THE MOULDINGS
I RECKON KUBRICK WAS KIND MAN AND IM A FAN OF THE FACEMAN
WITH NO SPACE IN THIS SPACEJAM NO ONE HAS SEEN US
VENUS WAS A BOY AND IN NOT MAKING THE NIGHT MOVES
AT TIMES THE SAUCER IS SPINNING TO MEET MR ZARKOV
THIS ORBIT IS CAUSING A SYSTEMIC SHADOW
MORE LAZY THAN LAZERS ON AN ALIEN
I AM NOT A SPACEMAN BUT I M SOON GOING BE ONE
MORE ENTERPRISE THAN A DAY ON THE DARK SIDE
ITS JUST AMAZING WHAT STARGAZING WILL BRING YOU
WITH AN EXTRA TERRESTRIAL IN MY GARDEN TO SING TO

School Daze

When I was a boy I found joy with a toy and also,

Played games and sprayed our names on walls down lanes,

And when the rains came found drains to play our tunes on.

We had our heads in the clouds at school, we had delusions about exclusions,

And no solutions for the confusions.

They tried to teach us and preach to us but couldn't reach us with their pathetic arithmetic and

Fried our brains and Like trains kept going on and on and on.

My mate had a slap-happy pappy and no mum to change the nappy.

His best alliance was in science and he was the experiment that went so horribly wrong.

The song wasn't long but our words were all hidden and fun was forbidden in the grand hall of fame,

So the clock ticks in dismay at the boy aged six who throws bricks and sticks on the road,

But when time and crime are more sublime than the rhyme that don't rhyme,

So for now I'm leaning on life's lamppost and seeing the rules are for fools who don't have tools,

To fix the fixation of one nation, stabbing and grabbing at mortality and fame.

They shoot us and pollute us with their lies and as time flies things don't change.

It's my mission to find a new position and take the decision to go to their prison,

Where angels can fly and I'm going to try and take us before they can break us and make us,

And you and me can be free and make poetry and bring calm to this world eventually...

Cartoon Capers

I really, really love Scooby Dooby Doo,

Hong Kong Phooey, Donald Duck, Roadrunner too.

Tom and Jerry, Daffy Duck, Sylvester the Cat,

Elmer Fudd in his funny hat.

Tweety Bird, Porky Pig, Yosemite Sam,

Wile E. Coyote and Pink Panther was glam,

'If it wasn't for those blasted kids!'

Top Cat and friends lived under bin lids.

Barney and Fred, Wilma and Betty.

I watched my cartoons whilst eating spaghetti.

Foghorn Leghorn, Speedy Gonzalez was drunk,

Pepe Le Pew, the ultimate skunk,

The Tasmanian devil and Gustavo were great,

Granny always was in a state.

Marvin the Martian and Tina Russo,

Popeye, Woody Woodpecker and Mr Magoo.

Great Grape Ape, Dick Dastardly, Muttley and crew,

Anthill Mob and Penelope Pitstop,

To name but a few.

The list goes on so I don't mind if I do,

Share this moment especially with you.

THE TARGET

FLUFF UP THE PARKAS, POLISH YOUR LOAFERS,
JUMP ON YOUR VESPAS, JUMP OFF YOUR SOFAS.
DUST UP YOUR DMs, WE'RE HEADING SOUTH,
WITH A TASTE OF VICTORY LEFT IN THE MOUTH.
LET'S FLY TO BRIGHTON, THEN MARGATE, WE'RE SPEEDING,
THE PASSIONS ON PAVEMENTS WHERE SOMEONE LIES BLEEDING.
THE TARGET IS ROUNDED AND THE TARGET IS CLEAR,
ITS ALL POLISHED UP WITH A FAG AND A BEER.
WE'RE THE AUTOMATIC AMPHETAMINE BAND,
WITH BLOOD ON OUR HANDS AND OUR WHEELS IN THE SAND.
WE ARE THE RUNNERS AND WE'RE COMING FOR YOU,
THE MODS V THE ROCKERS HAS A HEADLINE OR TWO.
THE FRED PERRY AND TRILBY, AN IDENTITY BORN,
THE LAMBRETTAS ARE READY, WE FIGHT UNTIL DAWN.
THE PEOPLE DONT GET IT, THEY THINK WE'RE ALL STRANGE,
WE POLISH OUR MIRRORS OUTSIDE THE UNEMPLOYMENT EXCHANGE.
WE LOVE NORTHERN SOUL: THE WHO AND THE JAM MOVE OUR FEET,
WE HANG IN THE KINGS ROAD AND CARNABY STREET.
PRINCE BUSTER, SMALL FACES AND SKA ON OUR LIPS,
TATTOOS ARE COOL AND I'M MODERNIST.
SO LISTEN UP, LEATHERS, COS YOU'RE ON THE RUN,
IT'S TIME TO SLING DECKCHAIRS, THIS WILL BE FUN.
WE LIVE ON THE TWO-STROKE, THE TWO TONE ADRENALIN JUNKIES,
WEVE COME FOR THE ROCKERS WE'RE SWINGING LIKE MONKEYS.
TWIGGY AND BLUEBEAT AND WE'RE POPPING PILLS,
LIGHT UP ANOTHER AND HEAD FOR THE HILLS.
WE WATCH QUADROPHENIA WITH A STING IN THE TALE,
THE RIOTS ARE COMING, I'LL SEE YOU IN JAIL.
RUDE BOYS ROCK UP, HEADING FOR GLORY,
BLACK AND WHITE MINIS, ANOTHER LAD'S A STORY.
THE SHOUT GOES OUT: "WE ARE THE MODS,
WE ARE HERE, WE ARE THE GODS!"
DALTREY AND TOWNSEND SET THE PLACES ON FIRE,
UNDER THE PIER, FACES FULL OF DESIRE.
WE ARRIVE ON THE SEAFRONT WITH WIND THROUGH OUR HAIR,
THE COPPERS ARE READY, OUR POCKETS ARE BARE.
A BRITISH INVASION WITH RED WHITE AND BLUE,
IM HITTING THE TARGET,
AND THE TARGET IS YOU!

RUBBER DUCKS

RUBBER DUCKS ARE NOT RUBBER,
THEY ARE DUCKS AND THAT'S A FACT.
IF ALL THE DUCKS WERE RUBBER,
THEY WOULD MAKE A PACT.
AND CALL US PLASTIC PEOPLE,
BECAUSE WE HAVE SOME JUST LIKE THAT.
IN FACT THERE ARE A FEW AND THAT REALLY, REALLY SUCKS,
I DON'T BELIEVE A WORD BUT I DO BELIEVE IN DUCKS.
SO NEXT TIME YOU TAKE A DUCK AND PUT IN YOUR BATH,
SAY "I KNOW YOU'RE NOT REALLY RUBBER,"
AND PLAY AND HAVE A LAUGH.
SAY "I LOVE YOU" TO YOUR DUCK,
SOME MAY THINK YOU'RE COMPLETELY BONKERS,
ITS PROBABLY COS THEY ARE PLASTIC,
OR JUST QUITE SIMPLY PLONKERS.
IT REALLY IS A SHAME THAT NOTHING RHYMES WITH DUCK,
OR IS IT SIMPLY RUBBER THAT RUBBED OUT ALL THE LUCK.

PUG

THERE ONCE WAS A SLUG AND A PUG ON A RUG
AND THEY WENT TO SEA ON A TUG
ALTHOUGH IT WAS FOGGY
THE SLUG AND THE DOGGY
ALL SANK WHILST HAVING A HUG

SO THE CAT WITH THE HAT AND THE RAT
WENT TO SEA ON A MAT
BUT AMONGST ALL THE THUNDER
THEY TOO ALL WENT UNDER
AND IM SORRY TO SAY THAT WAS THAT

ALONG CAME THE PIG WHO WAS BIG
WENT TO SEA ON A RIG
HE RESCUED THEM ALL
AND THEY ALL WENT TO THE BALL
ALL WEARING A VERY STRANGE WIG

YOU'RE THERE WHEN I WAKE,
YOU'RE THERE WHEN I SLEEP
YOU WARM THE COLD DAYS,
YOU'RE MY THOUGHTS THAT I KEEP.
AS YOU WALK BESIDE ME INTO THE LIGHT,
YOU ARE THE WRONG THAT ALWAYS FEELS RIGHT.
THERE'S NOT ONE POSSESSION THAT I WOULDN'T GIVE TO YOU,
THERE'S NO END OF WORDS I WOULDN'T SAY TO YOU .
THERE ARE NO SECRETS I WOULDN'T KEEP FROM YOU,
THERE'S NO BEAT IN MY HEART THAT I HAVE LEFT FOR YOU.
THAT DANCE WE HAD WAS OUR LAST,
AS WE TURN OUR FUTURE INTO THE PAST.
YOU'RE MY PARIS WITH A SIMPLE GLASS OF RED WINE,
YOU'RE MY SHADE AROUND SUMMERTIME.
YOU GIVE LIFE WHEN ALL HOPE IS LOST.
YOU SPEND TIME WHATEVER THE COST.
YOU ARE THE BLOOD THAT RUNS THROUGH MY VEINS,
YOU ARE THE CHILD THAT JOINS IN MY GAMES.
YOU ARE THE FACE WITH A BEAUTIFUL SMILE,
YOU GIVE ME STRENGTH TO GO AN EXTRA MILE.
YOU GIVE ME SHELTER FROM THE WIND AND THE RAIN,
YOU ARE MY PLEASURE WHEN I'M IN PAIN.
YOU ARE MY GUIDING LIGHT,
YOU ARE THE WRONG THAT MAKES IT ALRIGHT.
YOU ARE EVERYTHING TO ME,
YOU ARE MY SWEET POETRY.

MRS MOP

Mrs Mop Likes her HIP-HOP
Goes **SLIP SLOP** in her **FLIP FLOPS**
always tip top, never **DRIP DROP**
Heels go **CLIP CLOP**, drops a bar,
like a **PLIP PLOP** on a **TIP TOP**
thats **MRS MOP**, don't stop,
job's **DONE.**

THIS IS MY SHED

This is where I go to bed,
This is where I watch X Factor,
This is where I built a thermonuclear reactor.
This is where I do my art,
This is where I play the part.
This is the place that's full of clutter,
This is where I hear people mutter.
Words of race/religion and hypocrisy.
This is the place that's home to me,
This is the place where I can be who I want,
This is the place where you just can't,
Swing a cat or have a party.
This is the place where I can smartly,
Write down things that get on my nerves,
This is the place where no one deserves to be.
Except when making poetree.

Confectionary

I have a slight confession,
About my confectionary collection.
It all started with Mum's little treats,
Now my Metro tweets are all about the retro sweets.
Would climb a mountain for a sherbet fountain,
Eat a fizzy wiz whilst reading Viz.
My blackjack and fruity salad chews to dye your tongue,
Down the Greyhound stores when we were young.
Pear drops and lemon pops from corner shops,
Cola cubes and cola bottles, mmm delicious.
Popping bubbles with bubbly and Bubblicious,
Flying saucers, banana and pinky shrimps,
Giant gobstoppers were not for wimps.
Chewy milk bottles, drumsticks were worse,
Liguorice allsorts, liguorice laces,
You should see the look on your faces.
Love-hearts were my terms of endearment,
Juicy Fruit yellow and my favourite, spearmint.
Refreshers, wine gums, all cutting the mustard,
Dib Dabs, candy fags, rhubarb and custard.
Choccy and lime suckers, humbugs and Smarties,
Parma violets were the best thing at parties.
False teeth were funny and all the rage.
Sweet tobacco paper, then we turn the page.
In the cinema, now Pick 'n' Mix,
Can't wait for my next Haribo fix.
Spangles, double dip and aniseed balls,
Chewits, Wham and lollypops,
Dippers, fried eggs and then the penny drops.
Chewing nuts, bon bons, candy canes,
these are the nostalgia games.
Dolly Mixtures, hard gums, collecting cards
Bassett tubes and pineapple chunks in schoolyards
Jelly Babies above our desks or underneath,
Eventually I lost my teeth.
So next time when I have some treats
I'm on the hunt fnr sucky sweets.
That's it I hope you've had a little history lesson,
And now maybe you can share your confession.
So now I'm thinking of what to have tonight,
With hand in jar turn off the light.
But before I go please do tell your son and daughter,
And remember to buy me another quarter.

HOLKHAM

WALK TO THE BEACH AND WALK A LITTLE MORE,
BREATHE IN THE FOREST; VIEW THE SEA TO THE SHORE.
TAKE A MEAL AT THE VICTORIA; SUCH JOY ON A PLATE,
SAMPLE A BREW, THEN MAYBE AN ICE CREAM ON A SLATE.
YOU CAN SOMETIMES SEE JOOLS AND HIS BAND,
THIS IS THE PLACE; THIS IS QUITE GRAND.
OBELISK STANDS TALL, LIFTS AND INSPIRES,
THE WARMTH FROM THIS PLACE,
LIGHTS THESE FRIENDLY FIRES.
MAYBE A CUPPA OUTSIDE WITH SOME CAKE,
THEN TAKE A BOAT FOR A RIDE ON THE LAKE.
THE LIONS STAND GUARD AND WATCH CRICKETERS PLAY,
THIS IS THE PLACE WHERE I WANT TO STAY.

THE DEER RUN AROUND FREE ON THE LAND,
TIME TO TAKE OFF YOUR BOOTS AND EMPTY THE SAND.
TAKE A BIKE RIDE AND THEN POP INTO THE SHOP,
A GREAT PLACE TO WIND DOWN; A GREAT PLACE TO STOP.
HUNTERS AND HATS, NORFOLK FOLK TREATS,
WAXEN JACKETS, PEOPLE TO MEET.
THE HOLKHAM POTTERY WHEN I WAS A BOY,
REMINISCENT OF A TIME SPENT WITH SUCH JOY.
WALK THE BEACH WALK TO WELLS-NEXT-THE-SEA,
RAZOR CLAM ALLEY CRUNCH FEELING FREE.
UPTURNED CRABS, TRANSLUCENT AND EMPTY OF LIFE,
BEACH HUTS WITH MEMORIES FOR ME AND THE WIFE.
TAKE TIME FOR AN ICE CREAM BEFORE THE PINE,
THIS IS THE PLACE THAT I WANT TO CALL MINE.
DOGS RUN AND PLAY, CHILDREN SMILE JUMP AND LAUGH,
YOU CAN FOLLOW THE DREAM, THEN FOLLOW THE PATH.
THE GRAND HOUSE LOOKS MAJESTIC, ROYAL YET INVITING,
WHAT A DAY – IT'S ALWAYS EXCITING.
A PURE PLEASURE CRUISE, BLANKETS AND ALL,
THIS THE PLACE THEY CALL HOLKHAM HALL.
RUCKSACKS OF DREAMS, SUCH SWEET MEMORIES,
JUST FOLLOW THE RAINBOW DOWN TO THE SEA.
PUT THIS FEELING IN A BOTTLE AND CORK IT RIGHT UP,
THE EMOTION COMMOTION WILL FILL UP YOUR CUP.
I WILL ALWAYS LOVE HOLKHAM UNTIL TIME DRIFTS AWAY,
I THINK I'LL COME BACK TOMORROW, WHAT ELSE CAN I SAY?
SO GOODBYE TO HOLKHAM, I'LL NOT SHED A TEAR,
BECAUSE I'M BACK IN THE VIC, HAVING A BEER.

LOVE LETTERS

If I wrote enough love letters
Then I'd be sure one would get to you
I could cover them with kisses
My lips would seal them true

This love I want to last forever
My heart searches further down it seems
My mind is full of your caresses
Time is taken with you in my dreams

As I sit and watch the teardrops
Fall slowly from your eyes
My anticipating lips
Await a warm surprise

If we should go our separate ways
Then id take a paper plane
I would wrap you with my arms
So I could hold you once again

If the heart is where my love comes from
Where will it go when it dies
Does it return to the heart where it came from
or will turn into the tears in your eyes.

If I could could write you my last love letter
and send it with passion and pain
I will remember the days we had together
Running and splashing through rain

When I see your face in the river
and as you drift away down the stream
You will always be with me as night falls
You are my strawberries and my cream

BURLESQUE

ONCE UPON A DARK MOON THE LADIES ARRIVE,
CORSETUALLY ENCOMPASSED AND LACED TO THE NINES,
DIVINE MAIDENS PROMENADE DEBAUCHERY WITH A DELECTABLE
DANCE,
FEMININE, ROUGED AND ELEGANTLY PLACED, GLOVED AND TATTOOED.
THE BURLESQUE CHANDELIERS OF LE CABARET,
ARMOURED WITH SPARKLE TONIGHT,
THIGHS ON SHOW FOR THE EYES TO CATCH,
SUSPENSE IN SUSPENDERS, RED LIPSTICK AND TASSLE,
FINGERS ON LIPS, RAMPANTLY CLASSY,
VON TEASING THE NIGHT AWAY.
THEATRICALLY POISED UNDER STAGE LIGHTS,
PERFORMANCES IN THEIR SINTELLECTUAL SIGHT,
VELVET AND VOLUPTUOUS BEHIND THE FEATHERED FAN.
THE AVANT-GARDE VAUDEVILLIANS RAISING THE DEAD,
MASQUERADING WITH THOSE MALEVOLENT EYES,
TWIST A TONGUE TO LE MARMALADE,
THE UNCOMFORTABLE THOUGHTS OF SEXUAL SERENITY
SKINS TRANSLUCENT AND PASSION CONSUMING.
A MUSICAL TRAPEZE, WITH EASE I'M HOOKED,
A MYSTICAL BALLERINA IN DRAMATIC FORM,
THE ANDROGENS PULSE AND PURSUE THE EROTIC.
HIGH ON THE HEELS AND HAIR DESCENDING,
DAGGER AND WEB PROTECTING THE INNOCENCE,
DREAMING OF A CARESS IN PASSING.
THE CIRCUS IS HERE, THE ACROBATS AND CLOWNS,
GREEN WITCHES AND GOBLINS SURROUND THE VOYEUR COLLECTIVE,
ONE SCRATCH AND THE LIGHT FADES.
TONIGHT I'M THE PREY AND I ALL I CAN DO IS PRAY FOR MORE.
LET THE FESTIVAL COMMENCE,
WITH VENOM UNLEASHED AND POISONS INJECTED,
PIERCINGS REFLECT PERPETUAL SMILES.
MY VANILLA-SKINNED LADIES.
GIVE ME THE MOULIN ROUGE,
LAUTREC IN ABSINTHE SPLENDOUR.
J'AIME LA BURLESQUE

TWO-TONE TONY

WHITE FRED PERRY, BRACES AND A TRILBY HAT,
RED CHERRIES ON, SKANKING IN HIS FLAT.
THIS IS SKA, THIS IS SKA, THIS IS SKA.
MOONSTOMPING BEATS DROPPING IN A DUB PLATE,
THEY CALL HIM SIZZLA COS HE PACKS THE RIZLA,
TONIGHT'S THE NIGHT FOR TWO-TONE TONY,
MEETS DOWN THE CAMDEN TOWN WITH,
ROCKSTEADY EDDY THE SKINHEAD,
GREEN AND MEAN SO THEY SAY,
ALLRIIIIIGHTA!
WHAT'S IN STORE TODAY IN THE VINYL WAY?
CHECKING OUT THE TROJANS,
FLICKING THROUGH THE COXONES,
UNION FLAGS SURROUNDED MOTHER'S PRIDE,
PROUD OF ENGLAND FOOTIE BOYS I'M SURE.
"TURN IT UP GUV, PLAY IT LOUDER!" THEY CALL OUT TO
JAMAICAN GUY, HEADPHONES TO ONE EAR.
BOBS THE HEAD AND WINKS,
"LOVE IT."
"GOT IT ON A 12 INCH, MATE?"
"CERTAINLY HAVE Y'NO!" IN A PATOIS FASHIONABLE
ACCENT.
" 'AVE YA 'ERD DE NEWS TADAAY, MAN?"
"NA."
"DE ISRAELITES IS NUMBER 1!"
"YOU GOT THAT? IT'S A HEAVY TUUUNE!"
TWO-TONE TONY TURNS AND LIGHTS A FAG,
ON THE FIRST PUFF HE SAYS, "STICK IT IN THE BAG."
HE THROWS ROCK STEADY EDDY A FAG AND, FLICKING THROUGH THE VINYLS,
CATCHES IT AND THROWS IT IN HIS MOUTH.
NOW WITH THE SPENDINGS DONE, VINYLS IN HAND,
LETS GO!
THEY JUMP ON A 279 BUS, HEAD FOR WALTHAM CROSS,

"LETS GO TO DEREK'S RECORDS DOWN THE MARKET.
CURLY SOO MIGHT BE THERE."
"I REALLY LUV HER."
"IS SHE THE BIRD WITH THE BIN LINER AND PINK HAIR?"
"YEAH, NICE!"
THE SKA ADVERTISEMENT AT DEREK'S RECORDS IS CAUSING A STIR,
ALL THE MODS HANG OUT DAAN THE CROSS AS IT WERE.
SKINHEADS AND THE LIKE KICK OVER THE VESPAS AND SCOOTERS,
WHILE THE COLLECTIVE CHESHUNT BIB THEIR OOOTERS.
" 'ERE, DEREK, STICK THIS ON!"
THE FAMOUS MARKET STALLHOLDER PLAYS NUMBER ONE,
ALL NOW SING "DE ISRAELITES A..."
CURLY SOO IS NOT IN TOWN TODAY,
TWO-TONE TONY HAS NOTHING TO SAY.
JUST SMOKES AND BOBS UP AND DOWN,
I THINK HE IS THE COOLEST IN MY TOWN.
ROCK STEADY EDDY WANDERS INTO SMITHS FOR A PAPER,
FORGETS HIS BAG, SAYS, "SEE YOU LATER!"
" 'ERE, EDDY, YOU FORGOT YER BAG!"
LIGHTER IN HAND, SMOKES ANOTHER FAG.
"ARE YOU COMING TO SEE MADNESS?"
REALISATION AND RAY OF SADNESS.
"NO ITS MY MUM'S BIRTHDAY ON SATURDAY NIGHT,
I'M GOING TO THE PARTY ON SUNDAY, SEE YOU THERE."
PULLS OFF HIS HAT AND JUMPS DOWN A STAIR,
"OI, KEEP YOURSELF SAFE, 'AVE YOU FORGOTTEN YOUR 'EAD?
IF YOU LOSE YOUR VINYLS, YOU'LL LOSE YOUR HEAD."
SO HERE IS A MESSAGE TO RUDY,
I'M THE RUDEBOOOY SO DO NOT EXCLUDE ME.
IF YOU WANT TO KNOW WHAT HAPPENED TO OUR TWO MONKEYS,
THEY ARE IN REHAB: A COUPLE OF VINYL JUNKIES
THEY MIGHT EVEN BE FAMOUS OR IN THE MEDIA,
I THINK I SAW 'EM IN QUADROPHENIA.
SKANKIN TO SKA, NEVER BEEN LONELY,
HE IS THE MAN
THAT'S TWO TONE TONY.

XBIGGYX

RED

I bought myself a red bus and with much anticipation.
It was in the sale at Harrods,
And saves me waiting at the station.
I took a ride to Redbridge and listened to the Red Hot Chilli Peppers,
I found a red post box to send them their red letters.
I also have a red van and wear a silly hat,
Some people even ask me "are you Postman Pat?"
I stopped off at a café and tried to Have a meal,
When asked for the red menu,
The waitress said, "I can recommend the veal".
So I ordered up my starter: Heinz tomato soup,
And when she brought it over I had a little scoop.
Cos I was feeling all red blooded and was in a sexy mood,
And when I asked her for her number,
She said get on with your food.
I usually have red snapper with a hint of dill,
It can sometimes turn my stomach and last time it made me ill.
So I ordered red steak for my main dish and asked for it rare of course,
I had the cheek to ask her if she had served up any horse,
I said can have some red ketchup and she gave me such a dirty look,
"Yes of course," the lady answered and picked up her red book.
"Would you like a sweet now or a glass of red wine?"
I said, "Yes of course, dear – are you coming back to mine?"
The waitress pouted up her red lips and turned a funny shade of red,
I said I would like some afters,
Then she slapped me on the head
I said I fancy strawberry jelly with a hint of cream,
She walked down the red carpet,
And said, "Baby in your dreams!"
I gave her a great big red rose with a red balloon.

She said, "Thank you for coming,
But don't come back too soon."
So I jumped in my red Ferrari and wore a red poppy on my chest,
She put on her red lippy and said, "Have you passed your test?"
"You seem to be obsessed, dear, have you heard of OCD"
I said. "I just like red things – that seems OK to me.
You see I come from a red planet; you humans call it Mars,
You can come there if you want to,
 But all people have red cars.
We don't have mobile phones yet,
So I use the red phone box,
And when I go to bed I only wear red socks.
I'm going to push this big red button,
And no matter what you think.
Cos now I've discovered Red Bull,
It is my favourite drink.
You have this thing called Red Nose Day,
So I'm getting my one from a shop.
So that I don't get caught red handed,
I am never gonna stop.
I've heard of the red light district,
So I'm heading there right now,
In The Hunt for Red October,
The Red Cross can show me how,
I love your Red Arrows as they leave red mist in the air,
I'll be back again at Xmas to see the red man with curly hair.
I'm going to try and dye his beard red,
And maybe give him fashion tips,
I want to give him a red jumper,
And kiss him on the lips.

MARILYN

THERE I WAS, FULFILLING MY ESCALATOR MISSION,
SO I JUMPED ON THE TUBE AND TOOK UP MY POSITION.
COMPLETELY BY CHANCE AND IN MY IPOD SLUMBER,
I DRIFTED AWAY AND COUNTED EACH STATION BY NUMBER.
WITH ONE EYE OPEN, COUNTING DOWN THE STATIONS,
I STARTED TO REALISE I HAD MISSED MY DESTINATION.
AND JUST AS IF THIS WAS MEANT TO BE,
THE NEXT MOMENT IN TIME WAS PURE POETRY.
THE MAN SITTING NEXT TO ME SUDDENLY PUT DOWN HIS PAPER,
SHIFTED HIS BAG AND SAID "SEE YOU LATER".
THEN MY WORLD WOULD COME ALIVE – SO
THE PERSON WHO SAT NEXT TO ME – WAS MARILYN MONROE,
SHE ANGELICALLY SPOKE WITH A WHISPERING TONE,
"I HOPE YOU DON'T MIND, I'M TRAVELLING ALONE".
YOU COULDN'T MAKE THIS UP SO I PUT DOWN MY PHONE.
I WAS SHAKING INSIDE AND MY HEART WENT ALL SILLY.
I ASKED "WHERE YOU GOING", SHE SAID, "PICCADILLY."
"I HOPE YOU DON'T MIND, I'M YOUR NUMBER 1 FAN,
I'M NOT LOOKING FOR TROUBLE, I'M NOT THAT SORT OF A MAN.
DO YOU FANCY A DRINK OR A SMALL BITE TO EAT?
WE COULD KEEP IT QUITE LOCAL, PERHAPS OXFORD STREET?"
SHE SAID, "OKAY – IN A RUSH I AM NOT."
SHE WAS DRESSED IN A DRESS FROM "SOME LIKE IT HOT".
I PINCHED MYSELF TWICE TO CHECK IF I WAS DREAMING,
THE SMILE ON MY FACE WAS INCREDIBLY BEAMING.
AS WE STOOD ON THE PLATFORM WE STROLLED HAND IN HAND.
"SO, MARILYN, I WONDER WHAT BRINGS YOU TO TOWN?"
SHE PUCKERED HER LIPS AND STARTED TO FROWN.
"I'VE BEEN LOOKING FOR SOMEONE LIKE YOU,
YOU SEEM A NICE FELLA".
AS WE HEADED OUTSIDE I GRABBED MY UMBRELLA.
"IT'S STARTED TO RAIN – YOU'LL RUIN YOUR HAIR!"
MARILYN SAID, "I REALLY DON'T CARE!"
WE JUMPED BETWEEN RAINDROPS AND BOTH GOT SOAKED TO THE SKIN,
WE LAUGHED JUST LIKE CHILDREN AND THEN WE WENT IN.
SHE SAID "SHALL WE SKIP COFFEE AND GO BACK TO MINE?"
I SAID "SURE!", WITHOUT HESITATION, "I THINK THAT WILL BE FINE!"
AT HER HOTEL SHE SAID, "JUST TAKE YOUR CLOTHES OFF!"
WITH THAT I CHOKED, IN FACT I STARTED TO COUGH,
THE BATHROOM WAS STEAMING AND THE SCENE IT WAS SET,
TRYING NOT TO GET EXCITED – AT LEAST NOT QUITE YET.

SHE SAID, "I'LL JUMP IN – WILL YOU UNZIP MY BLACK DRESS?"
THE NEXT BIT, IT ALL GETS A BIT OF A MESS.
I'M SORRY IT'S ALL A BLUR AND A HAZE,
COS I DIDN'T COME ROUND FOR NEARLY 3 DAYS.
WHEN EVENTUALLY I DID,
SHE WAS GONE BUT IN THIS LETTER IT READ,
"MY POOR DARLING, I'M SORRY I HAD TO LEAVE AND THERE'S MORE,
YOU SLIPPED ON THE SOAP AND BANGED YOUR HEAD ON THE DOOR.
I HOPE YOU FORGIVE ME AND I'M FEELING QUITE SAD,
I WILL COME BACK SOON – MY LIFE IS QUITE MAD".

"THE SHORT TIME WE HAD, WE HAD SUCH A LAUGH.
I'LL NEVER FORGET OUR TIME IN THE BATH.
SO I HAVE SENT YOU THIS – A GREAT PHOTOGRAPH.
THANK GOODNESS FOR YOU – I'M NOW NOT ALONE".

REFLECTION

This is not a true reflection of me,
The mirror, the image, the bits you can't see.
They say it's a science; a natural selection,
It could be a warm doctor's injection.
Who is the person, the form standing there?
What is the reason? An expression to share?
There isn't much rumination or time for cogitation,
There is only one face to replace a smile,
The place illuminates as you walk the mile.
Look into the river, the ocean and sea,
Is the person I see the real me?
When there is pain,
No time to be vain.
The crack, the stress, the violation,
Look forward not back, a mind-made creation.
The void I destroyed annoyed me,
The character, the actor, there is one benefactor.
The stage was set; the hole got deeper,
I'm now in hiding from the Grim Reaper.
Shadow of pleasure, your mind I can't measure,
The portrait, the picture, the hidden treasure.
This is not the true reflection of me,
This is the good, the bad is kept hidden,
The ugly stands behind me; the master forbidden.
Two sides to every story,
This one has one.

RECYCLE

Human – Numan
Gary – Speed
Demon – Angel
Delight – Joy
Ride – Horse
Race – Car
Passenger – Train
Station – Platform
Escalator – Stairs
Walk – Run
Tap – Hot
Cold – Front
Back – Side
Cart – Wheel
Bike – Cycle
Recycle – Rubbish
Waste – TIme
Clock – Hand
Foot – Arm
Body – Odour
Smell – Clean
Dirty – Grime
Rap – Poet
Words – Speak
Language – Human
End.

Poetree

I decided to plant a poet tree to see if it would grow,
It don't matter how long it takes, it might even be too slow.
I planted it with this in mind and so I could eat my words,
It might look nice in summer and I might even attract the birds.
My rhymes will be on the branches,
 My letters will curl up with the leaves,
My song will be here in springtime,
 That's what my heart believes.

You can sit and watch it blossom,
As the roots run and hide.
I can fill the sky with passion,
I can stand and watch with pride.
I want to stand within its shadow,
I want to feel pleasure, pain and joy.
I have watched it grow forever,
Since I was a little boy.
If it touches you with meaning,
And heals young and old and new.
I will simply grow another,
And give this one all to you.

HIPHOPAPOTAMOUSSE

I'M THE MEANEST THE CLEANEST THE KEENEST HIP HOPPER
I LIVE ON THE STREETS MY LOOK IS SICK PROPER
EMINEM MOVE ASIDE COS THIS BOY HE CAN RAP
YOUR'E LYRICALLY CHALLENGED AND I'M NOW FILLING THE GAP
A MONSTER OF RHYME A BEAST ON THE MIC
I DESCEND FROM THE BRONX BUT I HAVE COME ON MY BIKE
MY BARS ARE THE BEST AND I'M SPITTING TO TEST YA
TONGUE MOVING SO FAST ITS LIKE A PINK VESPA
AND WHETHER YOU LIVE IN A FLAT OR A HOUSE
I AM THE COOLEST HIPHOPOTAMOUSE
LIFE IS FOR LIVING I'VE GOT NOTHING TO LOSE
BUT I'M NOT STOPPING I HAVE GOT A SHORT FUSE
MY CHANTS REMINISCENT OF VERBAL ABUSE
MY AURAL INCONTINENCE WILL BE APOCALYPTIC
THE TIME IS RIGHT TO BE CRITICALLY CRYPTIC
I'M CRYING OUTSIDE BUT INSIDE I'M DANCING
THERE'S A CRACK IN THE WALL AND THE ROPE'S EVERLASTING
SO EASY TO RUN SO ILL RUN DMC
AND DO WHAT COMES MOST EASY TO ME
AND DISS ALL THE BOSSES FOR MORE COFFIN LOSSES
OPTIMISTIC IN NATURE AND DONT GIVE TWO TOSSES
YOU MIGHT HAVE TO LISTEN FOR THE SQUEAKS IN THE VOICE
I'M A MOUSSE WITH A MISSION AND YOU DONT HAVE MUCH CHOICE
BUT TO FOLLOW THIS MC AND LIGHT UP A STAR
THIS HIP HOPPER AINT GOING TOO FAR
DYLAN WAS RIGHT AND MARLEY A PROPHET
SO I CAN STAND HERE WITH BOTH HANDS IN MY POCKET
AND SPOUT OUT SOME LYRICS THAT MIGHT CAUSE A STIR
I'M THE GUY WHO WONT BE WEARING A FUR
BUT WHETHER I'M SLAMMING THE WORDS OR TRIPPING A TONGUE
I'LL BE HERE FOR ALL YOU LOT THE OLD AND THE YOUNG
I'M THE BEASTY OF BARDS I'M THE OLD TIMER THE RHYMER
SO WHY NOT LISTEN THERE'S NOTHING SUBLIMER
IAM THE FIRE YOU NEVER CAN DOUSE
IAM THE ONE THE ONLY HIPHOPAPOTAMOUSSE

SEA

The lapping of the sea comforts my heart,
The tide was in right from the start.
The sand on my feet gives hope in my bones,
The journey I take rolls around with stones.

The winds of change blow me away,
The lighthouse reminds me of a sunny day.
The love inside is wandering free,
The heart is carved on my favourite tree.

The driftwood dreams are beach and pine,
Then wondering when I can make you mine.
The days when we played were simple and fun,
The shadows we chased were born with the sun.

We find our reflections in the water,
And make our names upon the sand,
We watch time fly across the ocean.
As the mist covers up the land.
We follow in the footsteps of our fathers and our children follow too,
We cherish memories for tomorrow and make new.

Sometimes our minds are worlds apart but our hearts are one together,
We may need a bigger boat to sail through stormy weather.
The grains in the sand are rolling under my feet,
The sea is place that is my retreat.

The pinewood, the jetty, the time it feels new,
Nothing can better this time spent with you.
Kicking and jumping, I'm into the waves,
To be free once again not one of those slaves.

The smells of the nets, the boats on the water,
Make life complete with my son and daughter.
The fun and laughter. no sign of a tear,
You will sometimes find me alone on the pier.

Crashing and violent the storm hits the rocks,
Nothing but salt and sand in my socks.
The sea is my treasure, my partner my lover,
Something for you that's new to discover.

Watch Father Time race across oceans to reach me,
There's nothing that you or the teachers can teach me.
Experience the sea, lay down on the sand,
I will take you tomorrow so now hold my hand.

Let the winds blow all of our troubles away,
Jump in the sea, jump in today.
The castles are built, the drawbridges open,
These words are the echoes of lines never spoken.

Bask in the sun, raise a glass to the sky,
There's nothing to hide from so open your eye.
Put up the windbreak, let the kite fly,
Sit in the beach hut, watch people walk by.

The tide it has turned and is not coming back,
As seagulls fly over and plan the attack.
On your fish and chip supper outside on the wall,
The sea has the power and shall never fall.

Splish-splash go the children, I'm excited again,
I'm just disappointed I'm not one of them.
I'm happy here with my bucket and spade,
I've got nothing to help these memories fade.

So with crab-line and bacon I'm off to the quay,
There's no better place that I want to be.
My dream is a life, a life being free,
Away from the troubles – a day at the sea.

ALPHASPAGETTI

THIS IS MY CONFESSION
IT'S ABOUT MY OBSESSION
WITH WORDS
ABSURD I KNOW BUT THIS IS HOW IT IS
I KEEP MY DICTIONARY UNDER MY PILLOW
SO I CAN FIND THE RIGHT LINES
FOR NIGHT RHYMES
A RHYMING ADVENTURE
SOME SAY A POETICAL PIRATE
I'M NOT REMINDING THE P'S IN THE Q'S AND I'M SEARCHING
FOR TWO LITTLE THINGS THAT MEAN SOMETHING TO ME
SOUNDS SALIVATING AND I'M PROCRASTINATING MY REASONS FOR THIS.
A LOVELY LULLABY NO WOMAN TO CRY OVER THIS
DREAMING ABOUT THE LOVE FOR CONFECTION CONFETTI
MY DAYS BEING PETTY WITH THE ALPHA SPAGHETTI
THE REMORSE WAS NOT FINDING THE B'S IN THE SAUCE
AND I'M ON COURSE WITH A LYRICAL LIBIDO
SPELLING MY WAY UNTIL THIS DAY
THEN PUTTING MY REAL EYES IN
AND WAITING FOR THE VISION OF YOUTH
THE TRUTH HURTS AND
THESE ARE THE WEAPONS OF CLASS DESTRUCTION
BI LINGUAL BUBBLES BLOW THIS SHIP FORWARD
NO SITUATION NO PUNCTUATION NO CLARIFICATION
LETS LOOK AT THE SMALL PICTURE
LETS WORK AROUND THE DETAIL
COULDN'T WE JUST SAIL AWAY UNTIL TOMORROW
LETS SELL THE SEVEN C'S
WHEN YOU ADD IT ALL UP THERE IS NOT A SENTENCE TO SURF ON
THERES NOTHING GRAND ABOUT GRAMMAR
ITS ALL ABOUT THE WORDS IN THE WRONG PLACE
LETS FACE IT I'M LOVING THE ILL LIT TERROR SEA
FOR ME ITS OK COS IVE GOT A VOCAL UMBRELLA
AND THATS GOOD FOR THIS FELLA
AND IT'S VERBAL PROTECTION FOR ME SO
AS I SHARPEN MY TONGUE FOR A SPEECH NOT OUTSPOKEN
BEING TOTALLY TWISTED WITH BRANCHES ALL BROKEN
THE SENTENCING STIGMAS TO DROWN OUT THE DYSLEXIC
AS THE CURTAINS CLOSE AND I'M CUTTING THE COST
I TAKE TIME IN MY RHYME COS WORDS ARE ALL I HAVE LEFT
WHEN THE MEANING IS LOST
SO AS I RETURN FROM THIS VIRTUAL JOURNEY VIRTUOSO,
THERES JUST YOU AND ME READING THIS
IN A SUSPENDED SPLURGE OF SPONTANEITY
I CAN HONESTLY SAY THAT IT MIGHT COST ME MY POETICAL LICENSE
BUT WHEN WORDS DRIVE THE PASSION AND THESE LINES RAISE A SMILE
MY REGRESSION OBSESSION I'M NOW LOGO-FILE.

FLAT PACK

I ORDERED MY KITCHEN AND IT ARRIVED TODAY
PLEASE PLEASE PLEASE TAKE IT AWAY
COS IT CAME IN A FLATPACK
AND IM DOWN ON MY KNEES
I FEEL SORRY FOR THE THE SWEDISH
THEY MUST HAVE RUN OUT OF TREES
THERE'S 1000 SCREWS AND WASHERS IN BAGS
IM LOOKING FOR AT THE INSTRUCTIONS
LOOKING AT THE TAGS
1 ALLEN KEY TO DO ALL THE LOT
IT'S IN A FOREIGN LANGUAGE
I THINK IVE LOST THE PLOT
I'M TRYING TO HOLD IT TOGETHER
I GOT A GUN AND GLUE
I'M FEELING QUITE DEPRESSED
WHAT IS A MAN TO DO
I WANT TO IMPRESS THE MISSUS
I WANT NO IMPERFECTION
BUT IT LOOKS NOTHING LIKE THE PICTURE
IT'S A NEGATIVE ERECTION
MY CREATIVE STYLE HAS WILTED
IT'S RUN RIGHT OUT OF JUICE
IF THIS STUFF CONTINUES
I'LL BE REACHING FOR A NOOSE
MY KITCHEN IS GOING TO LOOK IMPRESSIVE
IT WILL HAVE A FEN SHUI KINDA STLYE
BUT THIS IS GOING BACK I'M REACHING FOR THE DIAL
I SIMPLY CANNOT COPE
WITH ALL THE FLATPACK STUFF
IT NEVER LASTS OR IS EVER GOOD ENOUGH
MY STYLE IS MORE DESIGNER
AND NOW I'M A CREATIVE KIND OF FELLOW
SO I THINK I WON'T GO FLATBACK
AND AVOID THE BLUE AND YELLOW.

BEING MUM

WHEN EVERYONE HAS LEFT YOU ARE ALWAYS THERE,
YOU HAVE THE BIGGEST HEART IN A WORLD,
THAT DOESN'T SEEM TO CARE,
YOU WERE ALWAYS THERE.
WHEN THE KIDS WERE THROWING TOYS OUT OF THEIR PRAMS,
YOUR TOAST IS ALWAYS BUTTERED AND SPREAD WITH LOTS OF JAM,
YOU ARE A SPEED FREAK WITH THE HOOVER AND ALWAYS SEEM TO CLEAN,
WHEN THE CLOCKS ALL STOP YOU ARE STILL THERE IN MY DREAMS.
YOUR LOVE IS UNCONDITIONAL,
YOU ARE SOMETIMES OPPOSITIONAL.
YOU ARE THE GREATEST MOTHER AND THAT IS SIMPLY TRUE,
WE GO THROUGH THE FOG TOGETHER AND AS ALWAYS ME AND YOU.
YOU GO OVER AND ABOVE, A SUPERWOMAN FLYING,
THERE IS NO ONE IN THIS WORLD WITH MORE LOVE THAN YOU'RE SUPPLYING.
YOU STILL HAVE A BEAUTY REMINISCENT OF AN OCEAN,
YOU SEEM TO THE HEALER, YOU HAVE THE MAGIC POTION.
SOMETIMES THE PRISONER, HELD WITHOUT THE KEYS.
SO I'M HERE TO LET YOU GO, TREAD CAREFUL THROUGH THE TREES.
A MORNING STAR THAT EVOKES A CERTAIN SMILE,
SKIN LIKE PORCELAIN, WEATHERING WITH STYLE.
SO KIND AND CARING, SHARING, ALWAYS MUM,
ETERNALLY BLESSED WITH A CONCRETE HEART,
IF YOU WERE ON THE STAGE, I WOULD PLAY THE PART.
YOU KEEP THE GRASS ALL GREEN AND ALWAYS LOVE THE FLOWERS,
I WANT TO GIVE YOU ALL I CAN TO PROTECT YOU FROM LIFE'S SHOWERS.
YOU NURTURED, YOU RAISED, YOU PRAISED, YOU GAVE,
YOU BATHED, YOU SAVED, YOU MADE, YOU BRAVED.
YOU HELD, YOU SQUEEZED, YOU TEASED, YOU FED,
YOU CARED, YOU SHARED, AND YOU SHED TEARS.
 I WILL LOVE YOU FOREVER, FOR YEARS AND YEARS AND YEARS.

WONDERLAND

COME ON A BUTTERFLY RIDE WITH ME, LET'S GET OUT OF THE CITY,
WE CAN FLOAT ABOVE THE NOISY STREETS AND FIND A PLACE THAT'S PRETTY.
I HAVE SEEN ENOUGH OF RAINCLOUDS, I'M COUNTING COLOURS IN THE SKY,
IF I HAD WINGS TO HOLD YOU THEN WE COULD SURELY FLY.
SO TAKE THAT BUTTERFLY, RIDE WITH ME, WE CAN FLY AWAY FOREVER,
WE CAN LIVE AMONGST THE MUSHROOM MEN, MAYBE WE CAN LIVE TOGETHER.
WE CAN SLIDE DOWN THE SPIDER'S WEB AND HIDE INSIDE A TREE,
PLAY OUR GRASS GUITARS AND SING SO MERRILY.
WE CAN SIT AT THE TABLE WITH THE QUEEN OF HEARTS,
WE COULD PLAY AROUND WITH RAINBOWS AND WRITE "DRINK ME" ON THE GLASS.
MAD HATTER CANNOT STOP US, WE ARE RHYMING AND A-HUMMING,
MR DEE AND MR DUM ARE OH SO BUSY DRUMMING.
I'M STILL TWISTING AND I'M FALLING WITH THE WHITE RABBIT,
I'M ON THE STAGE WITH ALICE, IF THIS IS LOVE I THINK I'LL HAVE IT.
SOME PEOPLE SAY I'M MAD – I'M NOT I'M TRULY BONKERS,
IF YOU REALLY WANT THE TRUTH, I'M A FRIEND OF WILLY WONKA'S.
SOMETIMES I'M GRINNING LIKE THE CAT AND SO THAT CATERPILLAR KNOWS,
ITS JUST A LETTERMORPHOSIS AND THAT IS HOW IT GROWS.
THE BUTTERFLY HAS FALLEN AND HAS DEALT HIS PACK OF CARDS,
IF YOU STAND BEHIND ME YOU MIGHT NEED A HUNDRED YARDS.
THE FIELD MOUSE AND THE DODO ARE BOUND TO HAVE A THIMBLE,
IF I RUN AROUND THE WOODS I'M GOING TO HAVE TO BE QUITE NIMBLE.
MY TIMEPIECE HAS NO TIME LEFT – MY HAT COST ME 10/6,
I CANT WAIT FOR TEA-TIME WITH CAKES AND BISCUITS.
IM FLOATING UPON DREAM CLOUDS THIS LETTER I WILL SEND
COS IT FEELS LIKE THE BEGINNING WHEN IT REALLY IS THE END,
WHO ARE YOU TO JUDGE ME MR BUTTERFLY AND MOLE?
I'M GOING TO SAY GOODBYE NOW AND GO UP NOT DOWN THE HOLE.

GOBLIN PIRATES

THE GOBLIN PIRATES ARRIVE PORTSIDE,
BLOWN IN WITH FOG AND THE TIDE.
EYEPATCHES, DREADS AND RUM,
TIME TO BE HOME FOR SOME.
RIDE THEIR HOGS TO A FOREST FAIR
HOLD THEIR CUTLASSES IN THE AIR.
PIECES OF EIGHT FOR THEIR GOBLIN KING
WITH ALL THE TREASURE THEY ALL BRING.
TALES OF BATTLES ON THE WAVES,
HEAD TOWARDS THEIR GOBLIN CAVES.
SKULLS OF MEN, SCAR AND TATTOO,
PIRATE GOBLINS HAVE JOBS TO DO.
DESCENDED FROM JAMAICAN LANDS,
NOW WITH GOLD WITHIN THEIR HANDS.

THROUGH ENCHANTED FOREST AND RIVERS GREEN,
STOP AT THE CASTLE OF THE GOBLIN QUEEN.
WHERE GOLDEN COINS ARE LAID DOWN,
AS A GIFT FOR THE ROYAL CROWN.

ON EACH AND EVERY FULL MOON THEY RIDE,
UPON LABYRINTH. LAKE, DOWNSTREAM THEY GO.
GOBLIN VOICES SHOUT 'YO HO HO'!
THE ADVENTURE BEGINS WITH MAGICAL MIST,
MUSHROOM HUNTING WITH A FLICK OF THE WRIST.
THE GOBLIN PIRATES MAKE TRACKS FOR THE FEAST,
WITH THE TABLE LAID AND THE HEAD OF A BEAST.
AS NIGHT FALLS THE SEA SHANTY DOES BEGIN,
TALES OF ADVENTURE AND THEY ALL SING.
THE GOBLIN PIRATES HUDDLE AROUND,
DISCUSSING MAPS AND THINGS THEY FOUND.
THEIR CAMPFIRE BURNS INTO THE NIGHT,
DAWN BRINGS FORTH AN AWESOME SIGHT.
UPTURNED LOGS AND EMPTY BOTTLES FROM THE NIGHT BEFORE,
DISAPPEARING SHADOWS INTO THE WOODS, HEADS FOR SHORE.
WILD HORSES RUN ALONGSIDE,
GOBLINS RUSH TO CATCH THE TIDE.
AND SO ANOTHER ADVENTURE BEGINS,
WAVES TO RIDE FOR THEM GOBLINS.
CAPTAIN BLACK GIVES OUT THE SHOUT,
THEYLL BE BACK NEXT YEAR, NO DOUBT.
SAILING ACROSS THE OCEANS FAIR,
OH HOW I WISH I WAS THERE.
GOBLIN CHILDREN NOW READ YOUR BOOKS, BE CLEVER,
OTHERWISE THIS TALE WILL BE LOST FOREVER.

JAWDANCE

AS I SKIPPED THE LIGHT FANDANGO,
AND ENTERED SLOWLY THROUGH THE DOOR,
I WAS FEELING KINDA WOBBLY,
TO SEE WHAT RICH MIX HAD IN STORE.
IT WAS A SPECTACLE,
IN FACT SPECTACULAR,
TO SEE THE COLLECTIVE CONSUMING THE COLLABORATIVE,
I WAS NATURALLY NURTURING THE NARRATIVE.
AN EARGASM OF AURAL PLEASURE,
A MASTERPIECE OF MORAL MEASURE,
AN AUDIO DANCE FOR AN AUDIENCE,
SOUNDS DANCING, WORDS PRONOUNCING.
LYRICALLY LATINO – AND YET PROFOUND,
TO FIND A COMMON GROUND.
I WOULD BE VOCALLY UNDRESSING,
IF GIVEN HALF A CHANCE TO JAWDANCE.
TONGUE TANGOED LINES CARESSING,
MY VERSE-SUVIUS ERUPTING AND SPOUTING.
OPEN MIC SPOKEN WORDS LIKE BIRDS,
FLY INTO SPACE, THE RACE IS ON.
APPLES AND SNAKES SET THE PACE,
I WRITE, I READ, I TAKE THE BAIT,
CANT WAIT, I'M NOT ONE TO SPECULATE.
BUT AS FATE TURNS AND TIME TICKS,
THOUGHTS EJACULATE,
C'EST LA VIE,
I'M UNSEEN IN A ROOM IN BETHNAL GREEN,

THE HIP-HOP MAN,
THE TIP-TOP TAN,
POETICALLY GLAM.
HIPPEST RAPPER,
LOOKS ALL DAPPER.
STRAWBERRY SUIT,
LOVING THE DREAM.
THE FILM IS MINE,
THIS RAINBOW CHASER,
TRUE ROMANCER,
A TRUE JAW DANCER.
NEXT TIME TAKE THE EARLY BIRD TRAIN,
RUN RIGHT THROUGH THE PAIN.
PAINT THE PICTURE AND LEARN,
CATCH THE WORM AS IT TURNS.
DJ TOASTING,
GREEDS A HOSTING.
NOW TAKE YOUR TURN,
VERSES BURN, THE HEAT IS ON.
IM GOING TO SCRATCH A LINE.
IN DUB SO LYRICAL,
WHEN I GET PHYSICAL.
IF I COULD POGO MY WAY INTO YOU,
IF I COULD PLAY THE RIGHT CARD,
I COULD BE YOUR HEISENBERG,
I COULD BE YOUR BREAKING BARD,
ANIGHT TO REMEMBER .
NEXT TIME, NEXT TIME.

XBIGGY ATTITOOD X

FROM THE FOXES POINT OF VIEW

I WAS SITTING ON A LOG CHEWING SOME GRASS
WHEN ALONG CAME THE MEN FROM THE UPPER CLASS
TO TELL MY STORY I WILL HAVE TO BE BLUNT
ABOUT THE GUYS IN RED FROM THE LOCAL HUNT
WELL AS SOON AS I HEAR THEM I WILL HAVE TO RUN
THAT DREADED HORN SOME CALL IT FUN
I JUMPED OVER THE DITCH AND STARTED TO SWEAT
THEY HAVE GOT ME SURROUNDED IN THEIR BIG NET
THIRSTY FOR BLOOD THEY CANNOT WAIT
HORSES ARE NEARER FACES OF HATE
THEY HAVE TAKEN MY MOTHER AND FATHER TOO
WHY DO THEY DO IT? I HAVEN'T A CLUE
MY HEART IS POUNDING I'VE GOT TO HIDE
THEY TURN UP ON SUNDAYS AND SAY ITS JUST FOR THE RIDE
OH NO THEY ARE CLOSER I HAVEN'T A CHANCE
EVERYBODY'S AGAINST ME IN A MAD TRANCE
THE BARKING GETS LOUDER IM GOING TO DIE
"THERE HE IS" I HEAR THEM ALL CRY
JUST LEAVE ME ALONE IN MY FIELDS OF GREEN
I'LL TRY AND LOSE THEM AT THE END OF THE STREAM
IT'S TOO LATE THEYV'E GOT ME BY THE REAR PAWS
THE PAIN IT IS GROWING WITH TEN SNAPPING JAWS
THE LIGHT IT IS FADING SO I CLOSE MY EYELIDS
MY TURN HAS COME GOD SAVE MY KIDS
AS I LOOK DOWN ON THE PLACE THEY CALL EARTH
TAKE HEED FROM THIS POEM FOR WHAT IT IS WORTH
THE RICH THEY GET RICHER AND THE POOR LIVE IN BOXES
PLEASE STOP THIS MADNESS
LOVE ALL THE FOXES
XXX

LOVELAND

THE ANGEL OF LOVE FLEW PAST MY WINDOW TODAY,
SHE TOOK MY HEART AND LED ME AWAY.
WRAPPED ME IN HER WINGS,
HELD ME SOFTLY BY THE HAND,
TOOK TO ME TO A PLACE
SHE CALLED CALL IT LOVELAND.
THERE WERE HEART-SHAPED HOUSES,
AND LOVE WAS IN THE AIR.
THERE WERE HEART-SHAPED CLOUDS,
LADIES HAD PINK AND WHITE HAIR.
DRINK FROM HEART-SHAPED CUPS,
FILLED WITH PASSION JUICE AND STRAWS,
RED LIPS AND KISSES ALL PAINTED ON THE FLOORS,
FLUFFY PUPPY DOGS AND PINK FLUFFY CATS.
MEN WITH HEART-SHAPED SUITS AND GIANT RED HATS
LOVE BUGS THAT DON'T BUG YOU – THEY JUST LOVE YOU WITH A KISS,
THIS IS THE PLACE THAT I'M SO GLAD I DIDN'T MISS.
LOVE SHACKS ALL AROUND AND I HAD A HEART-SHAPED BALLOON,
WHEN I LOOKED INTO THE SKY THERE WAS HEART-SHAPED MOON.
THE QUEEN OF HEARTS WAS SITTING ON HER HEART-SHAPED THRONE,
THERE WASN'T ANYBODY SITTING ON THEIR OWN.
THIS PLACE IS SO LOVELY, SO HAPPY AND NO SORROW,
I THINK I'LL TELL THE ANGEL I'LL COME AGAIN TOMORROW.
THERE WAS A PINK FLOWING RIVER WITH HEART-SHAPED BOATS,
A LOVELY CARNIVAL WITH HEART-SHAPED FLOATS
A LOVELAND FESTIVAL IS HELD HERE EVERY YEAR,
WITH LOVE HEARTS ROUND OUR NECKS, YOU REALLY MUST COME HERE.
ALL THE TREES HAVE HEART-SHAPED LEAVES AND THERES A HEART ON EVERY HOUSE,
THERE'S A HEART-SHAPED CAR DRIVEN BY A HEART-SHAPED MOUSE.
THIS PLACE IS FULL OF LOVE, I CAN'T BELIEVE IT'S TRUE,
THE NEXT TIME I COME I WANT TO BRING YOU TOO.
THERE ARE GIANT BUTTERFLIES WITH GIANT HEART-SHAPED WINGS,
THERE'S A LOVE SONG ON THE RADIO AND EVERYBODY SINGS.
LOVE STORIES AND LOVE POEMS ARE READ BY THE LOVEBIRDS,
THERE IS A CERTAIN LOVELINESS WRITTEN IN THE WORDS.
THERE SOMETIMES A LOVESICKNESS THAT COMES FROM A TRUE LOVE,
THE LOVE FAIRIES FLY ALL OVER AND YOU CAN SEE THEM UP ABOVE.
I WENT SLOWLY THROUGH A TUNNEL AND COULD SEE THE LOVE WAS DEEP,
I OPENED UP MY EYES AND KNEW THAT I HAD BEEN ASLEEP.
WHAT WAS THAT ABOUT? I HAVEN'T GOT A CLUE,
I CAN'T STOP MYSELF FROM SINGING,
LOVE ME, LOVE ME DO.

LOVE IS

LOVE IS SWEET, LOVE IS BLIND,
LOVE IS CRAZY AND IN THE MIND.
LOVE IS RIGHT BUT WRONG AT TIMES,
LOVE IS MAKING, LOVE IS TAKING,
LOVE IS WANTING, LOVE IS WAITING,
LOVE IS ALWAYS ANTICIPATING.
LOVE IS CHILDREN LAUGHING IN THE WATER,
LOVE IS SON; LOVE IS DAUGHTER.
LOVE IS HOT; LOVE CAN RUN COLD,
LOVE IS YOUNG: LOVE GETS OLD.
LOVE IS IN THE AIR; LOVE IS TO SHARE,
LOVE IS CARING, LOVE IS A RUMOUR,
LOVE IS HAVING A SENSE OF HUMOUR.
LOVE IS ALWAYS GIVE AND TAKE,
LOVE IS A PIECE OF CAKE.
LOVE IS LOST; LOVE IS FOUND,
LOVE IS FINDING A COMMON GROUND.
LOVE IS IN THE HEART; LOVE IS DESIRE,
LOVE IS WHEN YOU FEEL ON FIRE.
LOVE IS DEEP; LOVE CAN HURT,
LOVE IS LIKE AN IRONED SHIRT.
LOVE IS IN; LOVE IS OUT,
LOVE IS A NAME YOU WANT TO SHOUT.
LOVE IS IN PEACE;
LOVE CAN MEAN WAR,
LOVE IS BROTHERLY,
LOVE IS ALWAYS WANTING MORE.
LOVE IS IN MY SPECIAL PLACE,
LOVE IS FAST, AND A RACE.
LOVE CAN BE SLOW;
LOVE HAS NO FACE.
LOVE IS A LOVER,
LOVE IS ALL OVER.
LOVE IS HERE TODAY; LOVE HAS FOUND TOMORROW,
LOVE IS DOG, LOVE IS CAT, LOVE IS FLOWER, LOVE IS THAT.
LOVE IS SOMETHING NOT TO BE SNIFFED AT,
LOVE IS THE KEY: LOVE IS NOT THE ANSWER.
LOVE IS LUST; LOVE IS PASSION,
LOVE IS GOING OUT OF FASHION.
LOVE IS ME; LOVE IS YOU,
LOVE IS WAITING IN A QUEUE.
LOVE IS SOLDIER; LOVE IS SAILOR,
LOVE IS NOT A VUVUZELA!!!!!!

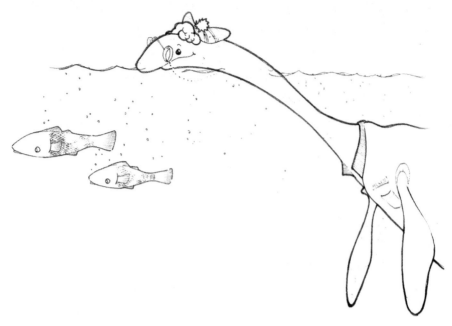

BETTY THE YETI

BETTY THE YETI WORE A PINK DRESS,
AND ONLY CAME OUT FOR THE SPECIAL OCCASION.
HE LIVED UP IN THE FOREST, WHERE HE SPENT HIS TIME,
WAITING FOR THE ALIEN INVASION.

HE LIKED FISHING AND CHASING BUTTERFLIES AROUND THE TREES,
HE WOULD HIDE FROM HUMANS BY SITTING ON HIS KNOBBLY KNEES.
HE WAS SUCH A LONER AND HAD NO ONE TO TALK TO APART FROM THE BIRDS,
HE WROTE POETRY ON THE WEEKEND AND COULDN'T ALWAYS FIND THE RIGHT WORDS.
HE WAS ONCE PHOTOGRAPHED RUNNING IN THE WOODS,
BUT HAS NOW BEEN ONLINE AND BOUGHT ONE OF THOSE HOODS.
HE WAS SHOCKED WHEN THEY CALLED HIM ABOMINABLE,
HE WASN'T INTO SNOW, HE WAS MORE AUTUMNAL.

HE ONCE GATECRASHED A W.I. EVENT — WE DON'T REALLY KNOW WHY,
HE ENTERED WITH A CAKE, HAD A TEA, AND SAID GOODBYE.

THAT'S ALL WE KNOW ABOUT BETTY BUT HE DID HAVE ONE FRIEND,
CALLED NESSY WHO WAS MESSY AND LIKED SCOTTISH SALMON.
THEY WERE BOTH VERY SHY AND COULDN'T MEET MR RIGHT,
UNTIL THEY DISCOVERED ONLINE DATING AND NOW THEY ARE ON IT EVERY NIGHT.

WHEN BESSY AND BETTY WENT INTO TOWN THEY NEEDED A GOOD DISGUISE,
SO THEY MADE UP AN OUTFIT THAT WOULD CERTAINLY RAISE THE EYES.
IT WAS MORE LIKE SOMETHING FROM A MOVIE,
IT WAS ALL THE RAGE IN THE SIXTIES AND REALLY GROOVY.
BETTY HAD A FLOWER POWER HAT, DARK GLASSES AND A WIG,
BESSY WORE A KILT, WHICH OF COURSE WAS VERY BIG.

THEY ENJOYED THEIR TIME TOGETHER UNTIL ONE DAY,
THEIR COVER WAS BLOWN AND BOTH WENT THEIR SEPARATE WAYS.
BUT LOVE PREVAILED AND THEY KEPT IN TOUCH,
AND TO BE HONEST IT DIDN'T TAKE MUCH.
SO THEY HAD A BIG WEDDING AND LIVED IN A PEACEFUL PLACE,
WHERE NO ONE COULD FIND THEM OR RECOGNISE THEIR FACE.

BETTY THE YETTY IS HAPPY NOW AND WALKS AROUND IN HIS PINK SOCKS,
AND BESSY NO LONGER HAS TO HIDE IN THE LOCHS.
THEY BOTH SPEND TIME ONLINE AND LIFE IS SO MUCH BETTER,
I HAVE THEIR ADDRESS IF YOU WANT TO SEND THEM A LETTER.

THE LAST I HEARD THEY STILL HAD THER HIPPY WAYS,
AND STILL GO OUT ON SATURDAYS.
DANCE UNDER THE MOON AND FORGET ABOUT THIER WOES,
AS FOR THEIR DISGUISES – THEY ARE A COUPLE OF PROS.

THEY COULD BE IN SCOTLAND OR TIMBUKTU,
OR MAYBE IN A NIGHTCLUB, MAYBE ONE NEAR YOU.

I HAD A DREAM

LAST NIGHT I HAD A DREAM,
AND IN IT I WAS DAVID CARRIDINE.
I HAD A BALD HEAD ALL GOOD AND PROPER,
NOW PEOPLE CALL ME MR GRASSHOPPER.
I WAS SHARP AND FAST AS LIGHTNING,
SO WATCH OUT COS IM KUNG FU FIGHTING.
I HAD A FLUTE AND A STICK AND WAS WANDERING AROUND,
I CAN CATCH A FLY WITHOUT MAKING A SOUND.
THE DREAM WAS GOOD, YOU COULD SAY FUN,
COS NOW I'M AN ASSASSIN, THE ORIENTAL, THE SHOGUN.
MR TARANTINO, BRUCE LEE AND UMA WERE IN TOWN,
I WAS CHOPPING THEM UP I WAS I WAS TRACKING THEM DOWN.
SUPER QUICK AND WITH A BLINK OF AN EYE,
I WAS THE GREATEST, THE POWERFUL, THE SAMURAI.
WITH SWORD IN MY HAND I COULD TAKE THEM AT WILL,
ENTER THE DRAGON, ENTER KILL BILL.
I WAS A CROUCHING TIGER FLYING THROUGH TREES,
AT TIMES I WAS CROSS-LEGGED, I THINK JAPANESE.
I HAD PING PONG BALL EYES WITH A LONG WHITE BEARD,
DO YOU THINK THIS IS NORMAL OR JUST A BIT WEIRD?
AND TONIGHT I'M HOPING FOR MORE OF THE SAME,
COS I FIND IT EXCITING, A BIT OF A GAME.
SO I'M OFF TO BED NOW, YOU CAN SEE I'M A FAN,
OF THE KUNG FU AND THAT BLOKE JACKIE CHAN?
I ALWAYS WONDER WHAT DREAMS ARE ABOUT,
SO WHEN I WAKE UP YOU BETTER WATCH OUT.
MAYBE YOU WILL SEE ME, I LOOK RATHER CUTE.
I'M THE WEIRD BLOKE, NOW PLAYING A FLUTE.

THE GRAND FAIRY BALL

TONIGHT I WELCOME YOU ALL,
TO THE GREATEST GRAND FAIRY BALL.
THE CASTLE IS READY, THE SCENE IS SET,
THIS IS GOING TO BE THE BEST YET.
SO QUICKLY, YOUNG FAIRIES, TO THE BALL YOU MUST FLOCK,
THE THEME THIS EVENING IS SIMPLY PUNK ROCK.

ENJOY THE FOOD, IT WILL ALL BE DELICIOUS,
I THINK I WILL BE THE AMAZING SID VICIOUS.
MY WIFE-TO-BE, WHOM I'LL SOON MARRY,
IS GOING TO BE BLONDIE – YES, DEBBIE HARRY.

PETER PAN, MY DEAR FRIENDS, IS GOING TO BE THERE,
HE IS EVEN THINKING OF DYING HIS HAIR.
HE'S NOT SURE WHAT COLOUR BUT BETWEEN ME AND YOU,
I THINK I HAVE SEEN HIM LOOKING A BIT BLUE.
THE FAIRY GODMOTHER IS BAKING SOME CAKES
WITH A MOHICAN WIG BUT HER TATTOOS ARE FAKES.

TINKERBELL THE FAIRY IS COMING TOO,
IN HER NEW LOOK I THINK SIOUXSIE SIOUX.
EVEN THE PIRATES ARE HERE LOOKING QUITE FLASH,
MAYBE THIS YEAR THEY'LL BE DRESSED AS THE CLASH.

WITH FAIRY LIGHTS TO LIGHT UP THE NIGHT,
I'VE SEEN SOME OF THEM, THEY'LL GIVE YOU FRIGHT.
WITH SAFETY PINS AND CHAINS IN EACH EAR,
LOTS OF BLACK, WITH WESTWOOD'S BEST GEAR.

THE KING AND QUEEN FAIRY HAVE PULLED OUT ALL THE STOPS,
EVEN THE PIXIES ARE WEARING PUNK TOPS.
THE ELVES ARE ALL HERE BUT I THOUGHT THEY'D FORGOTTEN,
BUT WHEN THEY TURNED ROUND THEY WERE ALL JOHNNY ROTTEN.

EVEN MERLIN THE WIZARD IS WEARING GREEN SOCKS,
AND ON HIS T-SHIRT IT SAYS THE BUZZCOCKS.
HE EVEN DYED HIS FLOWING BEARD GREEN,
HE WAS GIVEN A PRIZE FROM THE PUNK FAIRY QUEEN.

THE PARTY HAS STARTED IT'S LOOKING QUITE RAMMED
THERE'S A GROUP OF YOUNG FAIRIES DRESSED AS THE DAMNED

THE CHEF IS A BIKER, THE FOOD A LA CARTE,
THE WALLS ARE ALL COVERED IN GRAFFITI ART.
THE PRINCE AND PRINCESS ARE HOLDING A ROSE,
WITH ABOUT TWENTY PIERCINGS IN EACH EAR AND THEIR NOSE.

THE GRAND FAIRY BALL IN CASE ANYONE MOANS,
IS HAVING A BAND CALLED THE ROLLIN' OF STONES.
ONE FAIRY PIRATE WAS HOLDING A DAGGER,
THERE WAS EVEN A FAIRY DRESSED AS MICK JAGGER.
HE SAID I KNOW IT IS MORE ROCK THAN PUNK,
SO THEY LET HIM OFF AS HE WAS A BIT DRUNK.

THE GNOMES LOOKED RADIANT WITH LOVELY MAUVE HAIR,
ALL THE FAIRIES WERE DANCING WITH THEIR FEET IN THE AIR.
GRANDPA FAIRY HAD A VINTAGE STRING VEST,
HE ALWAYS LIKES A BIT OF A FEST.
BROWNIES AND NYMPHS WERE DOING THEIR BEST
TO LOOK LIKE THE LADY IN X-RAY SPEX.

MOON FAIRIES CAME FROM THE NORTH AND THE SOUTH,
THEY HAD GOT PUNKY TOOTH PENDANTS FROM A DRAGON'S MOUTH.
JIMMY THE CRICKET WAS IN THE BEST BONDAGE GEAR,
THE BEETLES AND BUTTERFLIES WERE SERVING GREEN BEER.
THE BEAUTIFUL ICE FAIRY WAS KEEPING EVERYTHING CHILLED
MAKING SURE THAT ALL THEIR GLASSES WERE FILLED.

THE BABY FAIRIES WERE ALL TUCKED UP IN THIER BEDS,
GRANDMA FAIRY WAS ONE OF THE BLOCKHEADS.
THE MUSIC FAIRY PLAYED ON MUSHROOMS WITH MIGHT,
THE GRAND FAIRY BALL WAS THUMPING TONIGHT.
 ALL EXCEPT FOR ONE LITTLE FAIRY WHO WAS LOOKING QUITE SAD,
I THINK SHE HAD LOST HER MUM AND HER DAD.
BUT WHEN FIRE FAIRY CAME TO HER AID,
SHE WARMED HER UP WITH A HOT DRINK THAT SHE'D MADE.
HER PARENTS SOON TURNED UP AND EVERYTHING WAS FINE,
THEY HAD PAINTED THIER FACES WITH SHAM 69.
THE GRAND FAIRY BALL WAS A ROARING SUCCESS,
EVEN FOR THE FAIRY PRINCE AND PRINCESS.
THEY HAD THE STRANGLERS TO TEA WHO SANG THEIR SONG 'PEACHES',
THE LEPRECHAUNS ALL HAD GREEN PUNKY BREECHES.
SO NOW ITS ALL OVER AND IT FELT LIKE A BIT OF A DREAM,
PERHAPS YOU CAN HELP ME CHOOSE NEXT YEAR'S BALL THEME.
I'M THINKING FIREWORKS BUT DON'T TELL YOUR MUM,
I'LL SEND YOU AN INVITE; MAYBE YOU'LL COME.

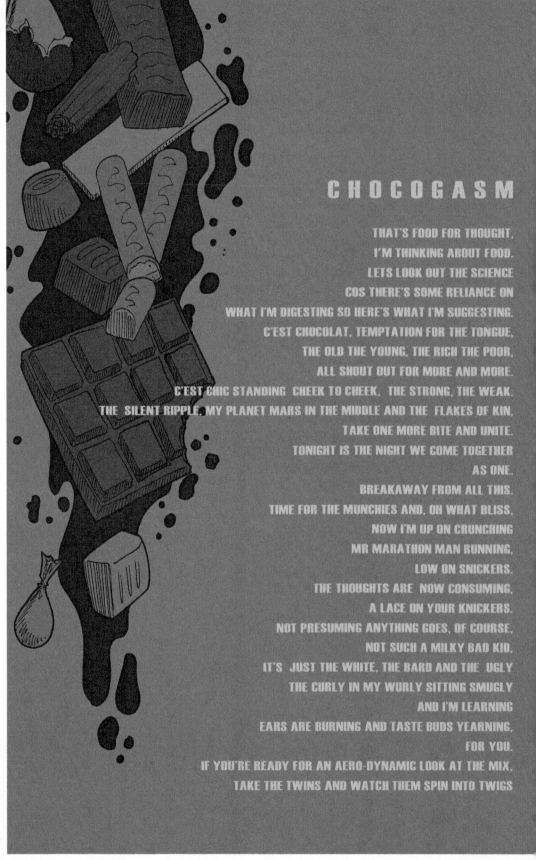

CHOCOGASM

THAT'S FOOD FOR THOUGHT,
I'M THINKING ABOUT FOOD.
LETS LOOK OUT THE SCIENCE
COS THERE'S SOME RELIANCE ON
WHAT I'M DIGESTING SO HERE'S WHAT I'M SUGGESTING.
C'EST CHOCOLAT, TEMPTATION FOR THE TONGUE,
THE OLD THE YOUNG, THE RICH THE POOR,
ALL SHOUT OUT FOR MORE AND MORE.
C'EST CHIC STANDING CHEEK TO CHEEK, THE STRONG, THE WEAK.
THE SILENT RIPPLE, MY PLANET MARS IN THE MIDDLE AND THE FLAKES OF KIN,
TAKE ONE MORE BITE AND UNITE.
TONIGHT IS THE NIGHT WE COME TOGETHER
AS ONE.
BREAKAWAY FROM ALL THIS.
TIME FOR THE MUNCHIES AND, OH WHAT BLISS.
NOW I'M UP ON CRUNCHING
MR MARATHON MAN RUNNING,
LOW ON SNICKERS.
THE THOUGHTS ARE NOW CONSUMING.
A LACE ON YOUR KNICKERS.
NOT PRESUMING ANYTHING GOES, OF COURSE.
NOT SUCH A MILKY BAD KID,
IT'S JUST THE WHITE, THE BARD AND THE UGLY
THE CURLY IN MY WURLY SITTING SMUGLY
AND I'M LEARNING
EARS ARE BURNING AND TASTE BUDS YEARNING.
FOR YOU.
IF YOU'RE READY FOR AN AERO-DYNAMIC LOOK AT THE MIX,
TAKE THE TWINS AND WATCH THEM SPIN INTO TWIGS

IN THIS COUNTY THE BOUNTY IS OUT JUST ANOTHER FINGER OF FUDGE IS
NOT QUITE ENOUGH.
THE TOUGHEST BIT IS ALWAYS,
EVERYTHING BUT THE TWIRL,
THE TIME TO FOOL AROUND AND MAKE LOVE IN A WAR ZONE,
THE TOBY LA RONE.
THE TEMPTATION TOO HIGH, TRIANGULAR,
THE SMART 'E', THE MANDEM RAPPER, THE TASTY TOE TAPPER.
THE MEOW, THE PURR IN YOUR VOICE GIVES ME NO CHOICE,
BUT TO LOVE THAT KITTY KAT SMILE BY A MILE. I'M YOURS FOR THE TAKING,
BUT YES YOU'RE RIGHT I'M THAT GEEZER WITH A MOUNTAIN MY TEASER TO PLEASE YER,
ALL THE WAY FROM ANOTHER GALAXY TO SEE HER.
NO ASSUMPTIONS ON MY CONSUMPTIONS,
I'M THE POETIC,
THE PAUNCH THAT MUNCHES FROM THE HIP,
THE CHOCOLATE CHIP OFF THE BLOCK,
THE TRIP HOP, THE SALIVATOR, THE TERMINATOR.
IM THINKING OF YOU AGAIN WET FROM THE RAIN,
TAKE A BUS RIDE, A DOUBLE DECKER AND FIND MY COMFORTING CARESS.
IT'S TIME TO CONFESS MY URGES AND POLITICAL PURGES ON YOU.
AVOID ME, COS THIS GUYS A PLONKER,
THE WONKIEST WONKER,
A MISTAKE, NOT A MISOGYNIST,
BUT A MISSED HONOURS LIST,
A SEXY SECRETION,
THE REASONS NOT WITHIN A SEASON,
MY PASSION REACTION IS NOT A TRUE REFLECTION OF ME.
YOU SEE MY GUT FEELING IS TRUE TUITION. AND NURTURED NUTRITION.
THE MYSTICAL MINSTREL, THE QUELLE SURPRISE, THE TRUFFLE, THE CAKE,
IT'S WHAT MAKES THE MOMENT GO MADLY YET SADLY.
MY CHOCOLATE HEART BEATS NO MORE,
AND FOR YEARS I'VE SHED COCO TEARS FOR YOU,
AND OF COURSE,
WILL ALWAYS,
LOVE YOU.
X BIGGY X

DANCE

DANCE FOR YOUR LIFE, IT'S AN INSPIRATION,
DANCE ALL TOGETHER, A COLLABORATION,
DANCE, FEEL YOUR BODY POPPING AND LOCKING.
DANCE AND BE DARING, TOTALLY SHOCKING.

I'M THE TRUE NATURAL DANCER, ALL FIRED UP READY,
I DANCEHALL CRAZY AND SOMETIMETIMES ROCKSTEADY.
I WEAR MY HAT ON THE SIDE AND I'M TWISTING AND TURNING
I'LL TURN UP THE HEAT AND GET YOU ALL BURNING.

I'LL BE THE JACKSON AND YOU BE THE STREET KID,
YOU'LL ALWAYS WATCH ME, I'M SOMEONE TO BE WITH.
WE'LL RAISE THE BAR AND PICK UP THE BEATS,
I'LL TAKE THE STAGE, FILL UP THE SEATS.

I WILL RUN AND JUMP OVER THE FENCE, A MAGICIAN,
YOU PLAY THE TUNE AND BE MY MUSICIAN.
LOCKED UP IN THE STUDIO 24/7,
YOU DANCE WITH ME AND I'LL TAKE YOU TO HEAVEN.

WRITE ON THE WALLS 20 FEET HIGH,
DANCE UP THE STAIRS TO THE CLOUDS IN THE SKY.
SLIDE IN YOUR NIKES AND BE THE DANCE MASTER,
I'LL BE WATCHING YOUR BEAUTY GROW FASTER.

YOU'RE THE ARTIST, THE ONE TWO-TONE BELIEVER,
THE NIGHTS ARE FOR DANCING, SO PICK UP THE RECEIVER.
PUT ON YOUR SMILE, TAKE ME AWAY,
DANCE UNTIL MORNING, DANCE FOR TODAY.

MIX ME DUB PLATE, STICK IT ON VINYL,
WATCH ME ON YOU TUBE, WATCH IT GO VIRAL.
BREAK EVERY RECORD, DANCE IN NEW YORK,
DANCE ON THE BRIDGE WHEN WE GO FOR A WALK.

DANCE ON THE SPOTLIGHT,
DANCE ON THE STAGE.
DANCE, BE THE ANIMAL,
RELEASED FROM THE CAGE.

IF THE GLASS LIES ALL SHATTERED,
DANCE ROUND THE SHARDS.
DANCE ON THE WALLS,
DANCE IN YOUR BACKYARDS.

YOUR FEET MOVE SO FAST YOU HAVE THE G FORCE,
IF YOUR MARRIED TO MUSIC NO NEED 2 DIVORCE.
A DEDICATION TO TUPAC AND BIGGIE SMALLS,
YOU'LL SEE OUR NAMES WRITTEN ON WALLS.

DANCE ON THE ROOF TOPS,
DANCE IN THE RAIN.
DANCE TO MY BEATBOX,
DANCE IN MY BRAIN.

DANCE, BE ROBOTIC,
SLIDE ON THE FLOOR.
WHEN YOU REACH THE TOP,
THEY'LL BE SHOUTING FOR MORE.

TONIGHT WE ARE DANCING,
SO WATCH MY FEET CLEVER.
TURN UP THE BASS MAN,
NOW IM DANCING FOREVER.

Rhymosaurus

I am the rhyme-o-saurus,
Hymn capable of a line or chorus.
No caveman but a brave man with a safe hand,
More sporadic than a Jurassic raptor,
Wondering if I should rap more through the trap door.
Ancient agrarian raptilian, civilised living librarian,
Not quite a huntsman, biologically archaeological,
Now with an axe to grind, with no words to shake a spear at,
More magical than a meerkat, and enough terror to take a black pill,
Fly with a terror Dac-till you can't focus, say hocus and stay behind me,
Be a diplo-mat not a diplodocus,
Be fast and run, run and hide behind at. rex,
If you see fire make, make a bee line and find your sea legs.
Watch the brave heart ride a brown bear,
Antique tongue taste a nightmare,
Bona fide bohemian on a lizard wing,
I'm the wizard king, making sparks fly high in the sky,
Spears to die for, lose one eye for you and I
For years and years we sail on stormy waters,
Sons and daughters, Flintstone family,
Lie in the rubble, too much trouble in the war zone.
Not vintage, volcanic or manic in a strange way,
On a bad day do a drawing, be an artist, make it minimal,
Taste the tarmac and beat the criminal.
I am the rhyme-o-saurus,
The one-horned, one-eyed giant in a swampland,
More words than you can throw a stick at,
Take a pickaxe and chop a tree down in a free town.
The ozone has long gone, tired of waiting,
I may be reptilian, rapping and raging and ageing into the time zone,
A fighter and a writer and a politician without the time to make the mission,
To the centre of the universe so I'll write this loony verse,
And put it in a museum with the old bones and bottles.
Aristotle was a drinker and I'm the thinker in this mad race,
And after all that do you think he saw us creeping?
Now I'm sleeping and dream-making,
Taking time out from the baking.
I wear a snake ring on my finger,
I am the bringer in of peace flowers.
I am the rhyme-o-saur,
Drop-dead dinosaur,
Feeling dreary about a big brain theory,
In the centre of a global tsunami.
Every arm has an army; every leg has gone barmy,
Take a spider in a web dance.
Forest dying; no food supplying,
Boats to sail on dragon's tail on,
People sending,

No happy ending.

BLAKENEY

A SHORT WINTER'S BREAK TAKES ME ONCE AGAIN TO MY BELOVED BLAKENEY,

AS I TAKE MY FIRST INTAKE OF COASTAL BREATH ON THIS FEBRUARY MORNING.

I WALK INTO A POET'S DREAM AND THE MOMENT ENGULFS ME LIKE A WARM BLANKET AT THE FIRESIDE.

THAT SALTY TASTE ALWAYS REMINDS ME OF A CHILDHOOD IN THE DISTANT PAST,

CHARACTERS IN CAGOULES AND WELLINGTON HUNTERS LAUGHING AND LOOKING INTO THEIR VESSELS OF HOPE, HUNTING THE CRAB.

THE MASTS STAND TALL AND THE SOLDIER-LIKE WOODEN POSTS MAKE PERFECT PERCHES FOR THE GULLS.

EVEN TODAY THERE ARE HARDY CRABBERS DESCENDING ON THE QUAYSIDE

AMAZING, I CATCH MYSELF GAZING AT THE SEA BIRDS OBSERVING AND BACON-BAIT DESERVING,

THE TIDAL SURGES, WATERS RISING AND BOATS EMERGING,

THE BOARDWALK BECKONS THE MORNING AND LIFTS ME FROM MY CAR SEAT SLUMBER.

ROPES CLANGING THE MASTS, THE BELLRINGERS, THE UPTURNED BOATS WEATHERED BUT WAITING FOR THEIR DAY TO COME.

WE START OUR COASTAL ADVENTURE AND HOPSCOTCH THE SAMPHIRE PATHWAYS TO REACH THE MUDDY TRENCHES.

UPON DRIFTWOOD BENCHES WE SIT AND SMELL THE AIR AND THEN PERSIST INTO THIS NEW GAME WE SHARE,

A RARE MOMENT OF CHILDLIKE NOSTALGIA TOGETHER,

THE SANDBANK SOLITUDE, A TONIC FOR PETULANCE AND PAIN.

THE REAL TWEETERS SWEEP PAST WITH BINOCULARS AS PENDULUM PENDANTS,

ALL GIVE WELCOME GREETINGS AND A NOD; ALL CARRY HONEST DEMEANOURS.

THE MARSHLAND MEANDERINGS REMINISCENT OF A BEACH HUT DREAM I HAD ONCE UPON A TIME IN A FOREST LIFE NOT THAT LONG AGO.

THE TIDE TURNS AND A SOLITARY SEAL FOLLOWS THE FLOW INTO TOWN,

BOBBING AND BASHFUL CAUSING A MURMURING FOR THE MARINERS,

EVENTUALLY, BREAKING THE BEACHCOMBERS' STARE,

HE DROPS AND DISAPPEARS INTO THE GREY.

A RUSTY BOAT PUTS A SMILE ON MY FACE AS ICE CREAM DAYS FLICKER THROUGH MY MIND

CHAINED AND ROPED TIED, PROTECTED BUT NOW I'M WISHING I WAS SAILING THE VESSEL VOLCANIC INTO A PIRATE CRUSADE.

AS WE HEAD BACK PLASTIC BUCKETS AND NETS PUT MY FAITH BACK INTO A WORLD AT WAR,

SHIP MASTS REACH FOR THE SKY CHURCH-LIKE.

FRAMED AND NOW BLOWING IN THE WIND, A SEAWEED MEDUSA CATCHES THE EYE AND IT WRAPS ITSELF AROUND MY MIND.

QUAYSIDE PORTHOLES ECHO THE BREEZE AND THE YELLOW LIGHTS FROM THE BLAKENEY HOTEL

DRAW A SHADOW TO WALK ON UNUSUALLY QUIET MYSTICAL AND MOODY.

BLAKENEY, TODAY YOU ARE SERENE AND PICTURESQUE SO I'LL SEE YOU IN THE SUMMER,

WHEN THE CROWDS COME AND DISTURB YOU FROM YOUR SLEEP

AN EXODUS AWAITS, FOR NOW IT'S TIME TO TAKE THE TIME WITH ME,

LIKE A CRAB I'M HOOKED, LEFT SPINNING NETTED.

LET'S MAKE THIS ADVENTURE LAST, SO HOIST UP AND SET SAIL,

NEXT STOP, CLEY.

DYNAMIC DUO

WE ARE THE DOUBLE ACT THE DUO DYNAMIC

I AM THE SMALL ONE YOU THE GIGANTIC

YOU HIT THE PAGE WITH PURE PICTURE PERFECTION

I FIND THE WORDS WITH INKJET INJECTION

YOU ARE THE ARTIST I AM THE POET

A TALENT TO BE WITH ALL THOUGH YOU DONT KNOW IT

I'M THE ARCHITECT OF RHYME AND YOU SCRIBBLE AWAY

I FIND THE LETTERS AND WIGGLE WORD PLAY

I AM THE RIDDLER YOU ILLUSTRATE

NOW TWO TOGETHER SOME SAY ITS FATE

YOUR QUICK ON THE DRAW DETAILED AND DARING

A TANDEM TO RIDE ON A PERFECT PAIRING

ONCE WE WERE ONE NOW WE ARE TWO

YOU PAINT THE WINDOW I JUMP WRITE THROUGH

THIS COLLABORATION IS LIKE A GIN WITH A TONIC

THE SPEED OF THE PEN WILL REACH SUPERSONIC

LAUREL AND HARDY ABBOTT WITH COSTELLO

I'M THE SHORT ONE YOU THE TALL FELLOW

YOU ARE HANDS UNITED MY LINES ARE WRITTEN IN THE SKIN

ONE WORD ASSOCIATION ALMOST NEXT OF KIN

THE ALLIANCE WE HAVE IN ART IS A COLLECTIVE COOPERATION

ONCE WE ARE LET LOOSE WE WILL TAKE ON THE NATION

ILL BE A RHYMIN AND A CLIMBING ALL THE WAY UP TO THE TOP

LIKE TOM AND JERRY WE WILL NEVER STOP

I AM HIP YOU ARE HOP

CREATIVE IN CRAYON

YOU ARE DESIGNING MAKING THE INK DROP

YOU SPRAY THE WALLS AND LEAVE THE MARK

I AM THE SILVER TONGUE SLIPPERY SHARK

TOGETHER WE STAND TWO PEAS IN A POD

YOU ARE ROCKER I AM THE MOD

DING WAH DILEMMA

THEY TOOK AWAY THE TAKEAWAY,

AND REPLACED IT WITH A BANK.

I REALLY CAN'T BELIEVE IT,

OH HOW MY HEART SANK.

NOW WHAT'S A MAN TO DO?

COME FRIDAY OR SATURDAY NIGHT.

THERE'S GOING TO BE AN UPROAR,

THERE'S GOING TO BE A FIGHT.

NO MORE STIR-FRY NOODLES OR YUMMY CRISPY DUCK,

I REALLY CAN'T BELIEVE IT – I'M RUNNING OUT OF LUCK.

NO MORE CHICKEN AND BEANSPROUTS OR STICKY PRAWNS FOR STARTERS,

I'M GOING TO BLOW A GASKET – I'M FLIPPING TORN APPARTERS!

I DON'T KNOW WHAT TO TELL THE KIDS WHAT AM I GOING TO DO?

I'LL HAVE TO POP NEXT DOOR AND TRY A VINDALOO.

I WONT BE ABLE TO DRIVE THERE – I'LL HAVE TO GET A CAB,

I'LL TELL YOU WHAT I'VE DECIDED,

NEXT TIME, METHINKS, "KEBAB!"

TILLIE

I'VE GOT A DOG CALLED TILLIE,
WHO'S REALLY RATHER SILLY.
SHES FLUFFY AND WHITE NOT GINGER,
I THINK SHE IS A SECRET NINJA.
ONE THING I WANT TO ASK,
IS WHY SHE WEARS A MASK.
SHE'S A BARKING SAMURAI,
WHO WON'T LOOK YOU IN THE EYE.
SHE SOMETIMES HANGS AROUND THE SHOP,
GIVES CATS A KARATE CHOP.
SHE MIGHT LOOK ALL CUDDLY AND CUTE,
BUT SHE WEARS A KUNG FU SUIT.
I KNOW IT'S AN ANCIENT CHINESE ART
BUT I DON'T KNOW WHERE TO START.
SHE'S GOT A GOLD JACKET WITH A BLACK FLAME,
BUT I LOVE HER JUST THE SAME.
SHES GOT SHARPENED, POINTED CLAWS,
SLICES THINGS UP WITH HER PAWS.
FASTER THAN A BULLET FROM A GUN,
OH WELL AT LEAST SHE'S LOTS OF FUN.

HOMETOWN

This is my hometown my kind of town
the town that ignores the poor
the outdoor man lies sleeping in boxes
the foxes lets see how they run
running scared
silent in violence
the big money makers
all take from the fakers
disillusionment that it wasn't right
to stand and fight for the right
but just tonight it might be worth more
as old man river lies asleep in shame
I'm not playing the game of fame
or placing a blame on the name
but watch and wonder why we went under
bullets and babies scream
through existence and my persistence emerges
the dog barks under the bridge of fate
i take the wrong turn and I am lost
the traffic plays the tune
under the shadow of the moon
a nation culturally divided
through mother misguided
black taxi stares back at me

with a lack of a destiny
gives delay in delivery
the edge of reason and rationality
capital of capitalism
the city that always sleeps and
feels closed for one moment
sharks and scandals outlive the vandals and make victims
leaving vulnerable cocooned in bags of tears
underground and with a numb direction
sleep in section warm injection without protection
slip silently into the night.
might be a typo hypersexual but my
non -winterlectual brothers and sisters
are paralysed by imperfections.
the lights and the sights for more eyes
shine with no money huggers just laundry luggers
on the brink of starvation
my social plagiarism is profound but spirits remain the same
drip dropping the poppers and watching the hip hoppers
graffiti hides the pain on trains and the rain beats a tune
on my back
I'm no royal fan but a man with mission to stir cameron
and the crony coalition to a different position
break out break beat the word on the street is unique
this is my hometown this is me this is overrated
but what is hated cannot be translated into words
as the world spins and you follow me into temptation
my nation is reduced to a drip drop a tap of tears
and for years i want this to be my hometown.

JOBS FOR DADS

I AM THE BOGEY MAN DESTROYER AND SPIDER CHASER,
I AM THE ONLY ONE TO FIND A PENCIL ERASER.
I MAKE SURE THE BED BUGS ARE OUT,
I GET TO EXPLAIN WHAT A PIRATE'S ABOUT.
I'M THE DOCTOR THAT NURSES YOU 24/7,
I'M THE ONE THAT TELLS YOU THAT IT'S OKAY IN HEAVEN.
I THINK OF WORDS LIKE BOO BOOS AND RING BELLS,
I'M THE ONE THAT TAKES THE BLAME FOR YOUR SMELLS.
I AM THE EXTERMINATOR, TERMINATOR OF BUGS,
I'M A HAIRY MONSTER THE ONE THAT GIVES HUGS.
I'M THE IMPERSONATOR OF CELEBRITY AND THE LIKE,
I'M THE ONE THAT FIXES YOUR BIKE.
I PLAY THE CLOWN AND YOU LIKE SOME OF MY ACTS,
I HAVE TO REMEMBER SOME VERY STRANGE FACTS.
I AM THE FINDER, THE REMOTE CONTROL MASTER,
I'M THE ONE THAT MAKES TOYS GO FASTER.
I TURN UP AT CHRISTMAS, DRESS UP IN RED.
I AM THE ONE THAT TUCKS YOU IN BED.
I DO MAGIC AND TEACH YOU ABOUT THE BIRDS AND THE BEES,
I AM THE SCRUBBER AND CLEANER OF YOUR DIRTY KNEES.
I CAN DO THE BIZARRE, LIKE FARTS WITH MY ARM.
I AM THE PROTECTOR, THE ONE WHO KEEPS YOU FROM HARM.
I CHASE ALL THE SHADOWS AND MAKE UP STORIES AT NIGHT,
MAKE PAPER PLANES THAT JUST MISS THE LIGHT.
I AM THE EXPERT OF NOTHING, THE TEACHER OF LIFE,
THE ONE THAT TELLS YOU, 'HANDS OFF THE KNIFE'.
I'M THE DAD THAT CAN RAP THE DJ MC,
I'M THE CHAUFFEUR TO DRIVE YOU ALL THE WAY TO THE SEA.
I'M THE ONE THAT GETS BURIED UP TO THE NECK,
I WALK THE PLANK, YOU MOP THE DECK.
I AM THE CHEF WHO PUT THE BEANS ON THE TOAST,
I PERFECT THE POTATO AND MAKE YOU A ROAST.
I LIGHT THE FIREWORKS AND WATCH EVERY FASHION PARADE,
YOU MAKE ME LAUGH WITH THE THINGS THAT YOU'VE MADE.
WE CAN PLAY SOLDIERS AND THEN MAKE CAMPS IN THE HOUSE,
I AM THE ONE THAT CATCHES THE MOUSE.
I PLAIT YOUR HAIR AND YOU SPIKE MINE UP,
REMEMBER THE DAY THAT I BOUGHT YOU A PUP.
I AM THE FISHERMEN THAT TAUGHT YOU TO NET IT,
I AM YOUR FATHER SO DON'T YOU FORGET IT.

THE DAY MY DOG TURNED INTO A CAT

DOG-TREE
TREE-WEE
WEE-SEA
SEA-TEA
TEA-ME
ME-OW
OW-COW
COW-NOW
NOW-HOW
HOW'S-THAT?
THAT-BAT
BAT-RAT
RAT-CAT
CAT-MOUSE
MOUSE-HOUSE
HOUSE-BRICK
BRICK-WALL
WALL-SMALL
SMALL-BIG
BIG-TWIG
TWIG-BRANCH
BRANCH-LOG
LOG-STICK
STICK-DOG
DOG-END

TATTOO

Rollo banks and hardy at sea,
Skipper the schooner in Hawaii.
Sailor moon under portside light,
Teasing men into the night.
Whispers like a parting ghost,
Who's the man she wants the most.
Sailor Jerry at the Harbour Inn,
Takes another sip o' gin,
With liquored breath and smoking pipe,
Likes his flesh to be ripe.
Aloha girls on the sailor's arm,
Sun will set when the sea is calm.
Norman Collins with this painted legacy,
Will inspire many more you see.
Old ropes twist on bough and mast,
Sailor man, you're here at last.
Mist rolls in to end their fun,
Rejoicing now the day is done.
Trade winds blow the nets about,
"Land ahoy!", up goes the shout.
Tattoo time for Betty Boo,
Not another drunken crew.
Bohemians sing shanties and slip to shore,
Seagulls cry and men go off to war.
Sailor Jerry now paints ladies of the East,
Some want beauty, some want beast.
No fear, no pain − just red and blue,
The shark is mine and yours too.
Sailor Jerry's girls are pretty,
This is the place called Tattoo City.

PLANET BISCUIT
(THAT REALLY TAKES THE BISCUIT)

I'M A STREET FREAK URBAN,
AND ALWAYS LOVE A BOURBON.
MY CUSTARD CREAM DREAM,
KEEPS MY JAMMIE DODGER CLEAN.
THE CHOCOLATE DIGESTIVE I'M ALWAYS DUNKING,
THE COOKIE WAS THE ONE THAT MY TEA IT SUNK IN.

I HAVE ONE THAT I OFTEN CRAVE FOR,
AND IT'S CALLED A PINK WAFER.
THE TASTE IT ALWAYS LINGERS ON A CHOCOLATE FINGER,
RICH TEA IS A CLASSIC BUT A NICE SUGGESTIVE,
NOT A MASSIVE LOVER OF THE PLAIN DIGESTIVE.
SHORTBREAD HAVE GOT HOLES IN AND SO HAVE OREOS,
GINGER NUTS ARE REALLY COOL AND SO THE STORY GOES.

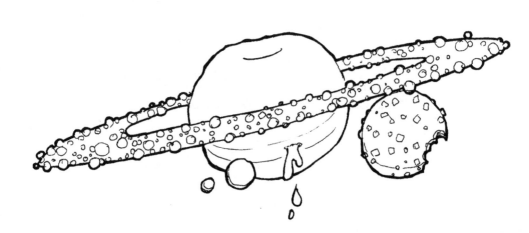

HOBNOBS ARE A TREAT, ESPECIALLY CHOCKY ONES,
FOXES ARE THE BUSINESS, REALLY LOVED BY MUMS,
MARIE ARE A LITTLE PLAIN BUT NICE FOR AFTERNOONS,
JAM SANDWICH ON A PLATE WITH SOME MACAROONS.
GARIBALDI'S GREAT WITH SOME EXTRA BAKE,
YOU CANNOT BEAT THE ORANGE IN A JAFFA CAKE.

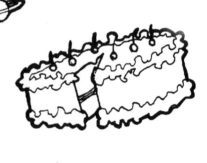

THE LINCOLN IS NOT THAT POPULAR AND NOT QUITE SMOOTH AS SILK,
I CAN SOMETIMES HAVE A GO ON A GOOD ALL MALTED MILK.
CHOCOLATE CHIPS ARE SPECIAL, ESPECIALLY WHEN THEY MELT,
I DIDNT REALISE THAT ALL THE ICE GEMS MELT.
THE VIENNESE WHIRLS AND CRUNCH CREAMS GET ME DANCING,
THE OATIE AND THE KIT-KAT CAN SEE MY TONGUE ADVANCING.
IF I HAD TO LIVE AGAIN I'D LIVE ON PLANET BISCUIT,
SO I'M HOPING THAT ONE DAY YOU COULD TRY AND FIX IT.

KIDS

KIDS DONT READ MUCH DO THEY?

IM NOT SAYING YOU GOT TO BE A KEEN-O,

BUT BACK IN THE DAY MINE WAS A BEANO.

AND A WHIZZER AND CHIPS, THE KIND THAT YOU DIDN'T HAVE SALT ON,

I CAN EVEN REMEMBER THE DAY IT WAS BOUGHT ON.

MY PAD WAS NOT AN IPAD AND I SWAPPED A CANDY FOR A DANDY,

INSIDE THE TARDIS WAS EVERY SCHOOLYARD KISS AND I PLAYED THE YO-YO.

NOW THE BOYS GET MUCH MORE ON PS4 AND I CAN'T SEE THE BEAUTY IN THAT CALL OF DUTY .

THE THUMB BOY THREE SIT AND TWIDDLE,

FIFTEEN HOURS ON A GRAND THEFT AUTO RACE.

LETS REWIND AND SET THE PACE BACK IN '73.

I WAS NOT A LEARNER ON A BUNSEN BURNER,

AND THE SCHOOL FLAME WENT OUT LONG, LONG AGO.

YOU SEE, I WASN'T INTO PHYSICS,

BUT IT'S NOT ROCKET SCIENCE IS IT?

YOU SEE KIDS DONT READ MUCH DO THEY?

AND I WANT TO FIND OUT WHY.

I'M NO MATHS MAN BUT BATMAN HAD A FLASH VAN,

AND ROBIN WAS NOT TWEETING BUT I'M BEATING MYSELF UP OVER THIS.

THE BASH STREET KIDS WERE MAKING NOISES IN MY CLASS.

BUT THE BOOKS TODAY ARE NOT WORKING.

THE TWERKING HAS TAKEN OVER AND ROY OF THE ROVERS LAYS DORMANT,

TODAY THE TROUSERS ARE DOWN AND THE TOWN IS EMPTY.

ALL THE KIDS HAVE FLOWN AWAY.

I SIT AND I SCREAM LIFE IS A WIDESCREEN AND WE'RE ALL ON WI-FI.

I HAD A HI FI WITH GREAT BIG SPEAKERS,

BUT NOW THEY'RE NOT SPEAKING AND THE VOICE HAS NOW GONE.

FOR ME LIFE WAS KERBSIDE KNOCK DOWN GINGER AND CLIMBING TREES,

GO CART RACING, SCRATCHED-UP KNEES – NOW I'M SCRATCHING MY HEAD,

WONDERING WHY?

I TOOK PRIDE IN MY VINYL COLLECTION AND NOW IT'S DOWNLOADED AND DONE,

BUT FOR SOME THEY DONT READ MUCH DO THEY?

WE HAD A BLACKBOARD TO WRITE ON: YOU HAVE A TABLET TO TALK TO,

WE HAD A BIKE WE COULD RIDE ON, YOU HAVE A TAXI TO WALK TO.

MY HEAD WAS IN A PARKA; YOURS IS IN A HOODIE.
IM NOT SAYING YOU'RE HIDING BUT I CAN'T SEE THE LIGHT AT THE END OF YOUR TUNNEL VISION.
THE DECISION IS OUT MY HANDS AND THE WALL HAS NO WRITING ON IT.
IT'S A BATTLE WORTH FIGHTING IN A DREAM SLEEP.
IF THERE'S ONE THING YOU CAN TAKE FROM THIS THEN YOU CAN READ MORE,
THE LIBRARY MIGHT BE CLOSED AND I NEED YOUR BRAIN TO FEED MORE.
EAT THE PAPER, EAT THE COVER, CONSUME EACH LETTER, WASTE NO WORDS.
DON'T INVEST IN TEXTING OR PUT YOUR TRUST IN A MOBILE WAY,
AND ESPECIALLY ON THIS BLUE SKY DAY,
TAKE YOUR HEADPHONES OFF AND TALK ABOUT THE SHARKS,
TALK ABOUT THE DAY YOU FELL OFF THE EARTH.
TALK ABOUT THE MONKEYS AND FOR WHAT IT'S WORTH
TALK TO ME.

WINTERS BREATH

The first light of day brings a cold touch to the nose and a moment to stop
and listen to the sound of car scrapers on windscreens.
Engines run continuously into the distance as small children walk
with a hand in their mothers'. Their bobble hats swing to the skip.
Cobwebs collect dewdrops like frozen tears on a lover's cheek,
Winter's breath freezes the trees and the crisp grass
 holds footprints in time sharpened by frost,
Branches stretch out like wispy fingers grasping onto to icy roads.
On this November morn the fireworks always remind me
of a distant past when they lie scattered and finished,
The cold mist rises up like a smoker's puff on the last cigarette of the day.
The pink sky stands still over fields and the animals look ready to move into the moment.
The drama of ice-filled streets starts with a robin on a fence munching
on a crispy worm, shaking every last piece of life, presumably long gone.
My last few moments to cocoon myself with warmth until
I have to make the journey into the world outside.
And as if nothing else matters I realise it's A rubbish day.
The monotony of this madness consumes me and as ever
I make haste with immeasurable layers of clothing
to hide my shame and dismay of this new day.
Two gloved hands come together and I blow a customary blow
to see my winter's breath in front of me.
The mirror-like puddles reflect an unknown body of uncertainty,
Walking slowly and with caution everything looks still and ready.
The leaves huddle together with a confusion of red and yellow holding on to the kerb,
Flowers curl and fold as to protect from danger of the dawn devils taking life from limb.
A distant siren brings life to my day and now time to think of others and their perils.
The last snail home brings me a smile to break the thoughts of danger,
As I climb onward I get a sudden nose full of fumes to remind me,
Yes I am alive today.

COLLABORATION

We are friends here so lend me your ears.
I'm here for you in spoken voice, a celebration,
hibernation time for this, the nation of mine.
As we all come together it's our destiny,
The meeting room, the observatory.
The world we look upon, we pull it down, we build it up,
The master's cup is half full again, the poetry of a thousand men.
Immortal words written in the sand, on the back of hands,
Scripts and scrolls on toilet rolls in undergrounds,
With hip hop sounds, beats and breaks, on boats on lakes.
In these surrounding lands where paper meets the pen,
Dancing together and who knows when the time is right,
Even if the fight is not right what's in me tonight,
Turn the page, jump on the stage and feel the rage,
Words depicting pain, inflicting and speaking with different tongues,
Musically and lyrically as birds are singing and I'm bringing you,
Into this art form, rise up together and weather the storm,
Collectively and in my tapestry come rap with me.
Let's come together and make a scene and with your serenity
of youth we can be as one eternally.
Let's drink to that.
In our orchestra the Renku is rhyming and with perfect timing
We join the bars, we link the chains and this collage stays the same.
The third voice emerges, the conception converges and gives life to the newborn,
The hybrid the harmonious.
Come taste the soup with us.
For one small moment in time let us put it all in a blender and return to sender.

THESE ARE MY INVISIBLE WOUNDS

These are my invisible wounds: The traumas, the torments lie hidden like cracks in the pavement, descending divided, a mother misguided leaves and deceives us with a moment of mistrust, in two minds colliding and collapsing closed curtains.

THESE ARE MY INVISIBLE WOUNDS: Today the play was not acted out but lies hidden – hidden beneath crispy cold skin, behind the fake smiles and lines made from the laughter of clowns yet depression sneaks in and now sewn in the subconscious through layers of time.

THESE ARE MY INVISIBLE WOUNDS: The lost sheep on the hillside has nowhere to hide but still he runs, runs into the dark divide. Broken voices, no rejoicing but voicing the moment he cries.
Look at the pain in the rain and the crashing of tears on my pillow, my aggression, confession speaks volumes to me.

THESE ARE MY INVISIBLE WOUNDS: Traumas locked away in a box, a toy box without toys – no one to share joy with, my words are there for you, words we can play with but no one to stay with.

THESE ARE MY INVISIBLE WOUNDS: The soldier lies bleeding and battered in tatters, a mind twisted, tormented, not as nature or nurture intended – the disordered stress stands tall but when he falls and he wears it like a badge, a gift given to please us and still those fragile bones lie shattered inside – the pride in his hands has no torchlight to guide him.

THESE ARE MY INVISIBLE WOUNDS: Broken backyards discarded bullets and a rusty blade left unsharpened, untouchable in turmoil. These silent lips speak through a pillow to cushion the blow.
This bruise of life has been blackened and once again my blood boils...

THESE ARE MY INVISIBLE WOUNDS: The faceless reflection shows no imperfection but you insist on a label to keep me in order. The code of genetics was written before me so you can assure me that they will try to ignore me. Down shadowless roads we meet and...

THESE ARE MY INVISIBLE WOUNDS: Water falls and the quill caresses all the stresses away, The swirl of each letter can make you feel better but for generations before and after the mirror lies cracked. So for these wounds to heal I am now making them visible. I am standing on the soapbox; I am standing to be counted, for I am a survivor but I have not survived.

My Mate Marmite

every morning about eight
i go to the cupboard and look for my mate
i like it especially with butter on toast
i probably have it a bit more than most
i love the black and yellow lid jars
i wonder if they have it on mars
i know some dislike it but i am not one
i have had my obsession since the age of one
it was a compulsion that stuck to my tongue
i have loved it on soldiers since i was young
dipped into the yolk of an egg that is runny
some people may laugh and think that im funny
it's black its gooey its a sticky it's gunge
 i have it in between a victoria sponge
a wafer thin layer spread perfectly right
i even get cravings in the middle of night
still love it in a sandwich with crisps with a crunch
i am a little ocd but still the best of the bunch
i got very distressed when the shop had sold out
so i started to hoard them so there was no doubt
i have hundred jars under the bed
another two hundred in the garden shed
i have some in the loft and im ready to feast
i cannot go without my extract of yeast
i went to the shops and noticed something quite strange
the little black jars were Nowhere in range
i looked up every Aisle but to no avail
the staff that worked there were as slow as a snail
so without hesitation i began my detection
i think i will need much further inspection
there were these little green men taking the jars by the score
 obviously aliens flying out the back door
they said they would reward me if i could supply them with more
so i acted all innocent and i know it sounds cruel
but i think they were using it as Their alien fuel
they were turning the jars into flying spaceships
i couldn't tell them i like mine on chips
so i left rather sharply and told no-one but you
the little green men into the sky they all flew
so i now look up to the stars at night
and still eat up my mate i call it marmite
i know you might think im a very strange fellow
but i do love the stuff in a jar black and yellow

TEA FOR TWO

I don't know about you but I like Typhoo.
She likes Earl Grey — what more can I say?
When there's tea in the pot,
I'm in with a shot.
Now some prefer herbal,
But I'm not one to give verbal,
To anyone with a cup of chamomile and honey.
And I know it sounds funny when the brew,
Hits your tummy and I'm not going to rattle on,
Just put the kettle on and get a teabag and place it,
In a china cup — that's it, or is it?
The chimps say "Coo-eel Tea Mr Shifter?"
There is always one in the pot for you my brothers and sisters.
The PG Tips the Twinings and all the rest,
Who knows what tea is best.
Some like to dunk; some like to stir it,
Some like it with milk; some would prefer it,
If it were pure with nothing added in,
Whatever I do I just cannot win.
So here goes, I'll try and be discreet,
Whatever the word is on the street.
I'm going make a brew or two for a treat not too sweet,
Some sugars or sweeteners or things added in,
Tea on tray: tea for today.
So which one — this will be fun,
There's the green tea, the spearmint, the peppermint tea,
The Darjeeling, the Chinese, the Japanese,
the morning breakfast, the infusions,
The Sri Lankan, the Indian the jasmine, ohh the confusions!
The organics, the oolongs, the rose Pouchongs.
The tea with a cake the time it takes to make it,
This is it, I can't fake it.
Whatever happened to the oooooos in Typhoo?
The bag, the leaf, the one underneath the pyramid, the square,
The apple, the pear, the raspberry, the strawberry, the tea at the fair,
The afternoon, the cream, the iced,
What the Xxxx is a Lapsang Souchong?
This is my song.
There's even the Yorkshire, the flat cap man with the cat flap plan,
 Letting the flavours flood out.
This is my shout, the lout, the tout the tea-totaller.
There's the lemon and gingers, the taste it still lingers on tongues.
 Some for the wingers, the ring-ding-dingers, the bell ringers,
 All take time for tea.
Ooh the aromas, tea for two, tea rooibos mates and chai,
And loads more — we are all getting high on the fumes.
Liptons luvvies, Brooke Bond buddies, tea pigs,
Tea and cigs, tea and coffee.
Black or white tea in bed, all in the pot together,
 It really don't matter — tea for the maddest mad hatter.
The strainers, the cosies, the roses, the vintage parties,
Tea and a biscuit, tea and toast, tea at the coast,
Tea in a flask, teas made, tea for you: tea for me,
Tea urn, tea cloth, tea in the afternoon.
Oh and when you watch it go round like a spiral,
Have a nice cuppa and make this go viral,
Tea with a paper, tea with the Beano,
See you all later — I'm off for a cappuccino.

STEVE BUCKLEY

I'VE GOT A MATE CALLED BUCKO,
SOME PEOPLE CALL HIM MUTTLEY.
HE DON'T LOOK LIKE A DOG,
AND I'D SAY THAT MOST ABRUPTLY.
HE IS A MUSIC MAN AND LIKES A KEYBOARD OR TWO,
IT'S A SHAME HE CANT PLAY 'EM,
COS EACH ONE IS SPANKING NEW.
HE LIKES A LITTLE A TIPPLE,
AND YOU WILL ALWAYS FIND HIM IN THE PUB,
WHERE HE MAKES HIS MUSIC,
HE LOVES A BIT OF DUB.
WE HAVE HAD SO MANY LAUGHS AND THE YEARS THEY HAVE BEEN KIND
SOMETIMES LIFE IS SIMPLY LIKE THAT, IT'S A SHAME WE CAN'T REWIND.
MAYBE WE HAVE SOME TIME LEFT TO MAKE A TUNE OR THREE,
BUT I MIGHT HAVE TO MOVE TO CORNWALL TO SING SOME POETRY.
SO BUCKO IN THE STUDIO, THESE WORDS ARE WITH YOU NOW,
AS YOU LOOK OUT OF YOUR WINDOW YOU MIGHT SAY WHY AND HOW.
DID HE MAKE THIS LITTLE RIDDLE WITH HIS PEN IN HAND,
OR WAS IT CHEAP ON EBAY? OR WAS IT Twenty GRAND?
THE SONG YOU SING IS PRICELESS AND I WOULDN'T CHANGE A THING,
BUCKO YOU ARE A LEGEND, IN THE WORDS OF MARTIN LUTHER KING.
OR PERHAPS A MISTER MARLEY, FREE AT LAST OR WITH JAMMIN',
YOUR LOOK IT DOES REMIND ME OF A TIN WITH SPAM IN.
I LOVE YOU ALL THE SAME AND NOW THE LIGHT IS FADING OUT,
IT'S TIME TO TURN THE PAGE COS THATS WHAT IT'S ALL ABOUT.
THANK YOU, STEVE BUCKLEY, A REAL TRUE LIFELONG FRIEND,
I BET YOU DIDN'T EXPECT THIS, ESPECIALLY AT THE END.

ACKNOWLEDGEMENTS

First and foremost, I would like to thank my wife, Sue, for standing beside me throughout my poetry obsession while I wrote this book. She has been my inspiration and motivation. She is beautiful in every way, and I dedicate this book to her. I also thank my wonderful children, Hollie and Oliver, along with our little pooch Tillie, for always making me smile and for understanding. I hope that one day they can read this book and also smile at the world. I'd like to thank my parents, especially my mum, for allowing me to follow my ambitions throughout my childhood. My family, including my in-laws, have always supported me throughout my career.

The late Michael Humphrey, for your encouragement and for making poetry cool. You will always have a special place in my heart.

All my friends and work colleagues, especially (the specialists).

All new and lifelong friends, and some still remaining on Social media, including the 'Biggyattitood' Twitter followers (all 600 of you).

Everyone at M-Y BOOKS; Jonathan Miller, for having the faith in my poetry, Chloe Hobbs, for the amazing additional artwork and creative ideas, and Kevin Saunders, for putting it all in the right way round.

A massive thank you to Daniel Rodriguez (illustrator). Without your fantastic pictures, none of this would have been possible.

Phil at Adapter Clothing, for kitting me out with my clobber.

Everyone at Jawdance and Forward Poetry, and a special big love to Bel, Rob and the boys at Griffin Marina in Norwich, for giving me the stage to perform on.

SCWBI – British Isles – Members – South East Region.

Thanks also go to Unilever, for your kind permission to use the Marmite Poem.

All the children and young people who continue to give me the drive and purpose to make the conventional unconventional, and anyone else that have contributed in some way.

LD - your ideas and amazing imagination have helped me along the way.

–Harry Baker and Mark Grist.

Everyone else that I have missed who is in my world or about to join – thanks and enjoy - SHEDS ARE THE FUTURE!

QUOTES

'SOME PEOPLE FEEL THE RAIN, OTHERS JUST GET WET'   - BOB MARLEY

'IF MY POETRY AIMS TO ACHIEVE ANYTHING, IT'S TO DELIVER
PEOPLE FROM THE LIMITED WAYS IN WHICH THEY SEE AND FEEL'   – JIM MORRISON

'IMPERFECTION IS BEAUTY, MADNESS IS GENIUS, AND IT'S BETTER
TO BE ABSOLUTELY RIDICULOUS THAN ABSOLUTELY BORING'   – MARILYN MONROE

'DON'T THINK ABOUT MAKING ART, JUST GET IT DONE. LET EVERYONE
ELSE DECIDE IF IT'S GOOD OR BAD, WHETHER THEY LOVE IT OR HATE IT.
WHILE THEY ARE DECIDING, MAKE EVEN MORE ART'   – ANDY WARHOL

ABOUT THE AUTHOR

Daren Peary is a poet and spoken word artist who resides in the hills of sunny Hertford in Hertfordshire.

He has been writing poetry for over 20 years and will release his collection in 2016, after a year of collaboration with local illustrator and artist Daniel Rodriguez in which they completed an amazing piece of work.

Daren first started writing poems as a way to escape the stresses of everyday life, and found that he had something worth saying when local newspapers and press regularly published his poetry.

More recently, he has had poems published in glossy magazines such as Hertfordshire Life and EDP Norfolk.

In 2015, Daren took the next step into poetry by performing his poems at events and venues in London and in the local area. One of Daren's most recent accolades is appearing in the promotional video for 'Apples and Snakes', a video documentary about spoken word and performance poetry.

Daren loves the various challenges that open mic spots and performing to large crowds bring, but feels that releasing a poetry collection will be a lifelong ambition fulfilled.

During the day, Daren works in education, and would love to emphasise the love that he has for poetry and for engaging children, young people and adults in this collection of poems.

He will be presenting an Introduction into Poetry for Key Stage 3 and 4 in 2017.

Daren writes from the heart, and has a rhyming style that is inspired by many different performers and poets, including John Cooper Clarke, Spike Milligan, Mark Grist and Harry Baker.

Daren is a family man, and lives with Sue, his wife of twenty years, and his two children, Hollie and Oliver.

He loves laughing, cooking, art, football, cycling, films and socialising with friends.

Daren's influences also come from his huge love for music and art, and he previously frequented the London club scene with the likes of Boy George, Steve Strange and Marylyn.

Daren loves punk, ska, and reggae, particularly Bob Marley, and has visited his home and studios in Jamaica.

Daren is a member of the SCBWI, and has a children's book in the pipeline for his next project.

'Lettermorphosis' is a poetry book with a difference, and he hopes that you enjoy the rhymes and pictures and that it inspires you to have a go, too.

Lightning Source UK Ltd.
Milton Keynes UK
UKOW07f1630131016

285202UK00014B/95/P